A MODEM Guide

101
Great Ideas for
Growing Healthy Churches

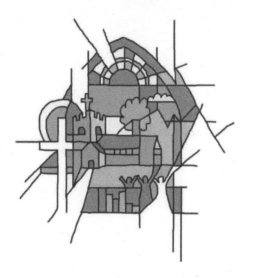

*A treasure trove of wise words and practical pointers for
leading and managing churches into healthy growth*

14.99

101
Great Ideas for Growing Healthy Churches

Compiled and edited by

John Nelson, Michael Lofthouse
and Anton Müller

CANTERBURY
PRESS
Norwich

© John Nelson, Michael Lofthouse and Anton Müller 2012

First published in 2012 by the Canterbury Press Norwich
Editorial office
3rd Floor, Invicta House,
108–114 Golden Lane,
London EC1Y 0TG

Canterbury Press is an imprint of Hymns Ancient & Modern Ltd
(a registered charity)
13A Hellesdon Park Road, Norwich,
Norfolk, NR6 5DR, UK

www.canterburypress.co.uk

British Library Cataloguing in Publication data

A catalogue record for this book is available
from the British Library

978 1 84825 045 1

Typeset by Regent Typesetting, London
Printed and bound in Great Britain by
CPI Group (UK) Ltd, Croydon

Contents

The Editorial Team

John Nelson is a founder member of MODEM. He serves as its national secretary and publishing editor. This is John Nelson's fifth book for MODEM as editor.

John was formerly head of the department of management studies and chairman of the faculty of accounting and finance, business studies, law and management studies at Liverpool Polytechnic, now known as John Moore's University.

John's management experience includes time with Rolls Royce, the National Coal Board and the Royal Air Force. John has also served as a management consultant to the Anglican Diocese of Liverpool where he worked with Bishop David Sheppard. He is active in his local church in Formby as a reader and chairman of the PCC communications committee and the regular church columnist for the *Formby Times*.

Anton Müller is an ordained Anglican priest. He has a passion for the mission and forward movement of the church through education and training. He has worked in ministry to visitors to Rochester Cathedral and as a tutor for the Rochester and Canterbury developing ministries programme. Prior to ordination he was the education and training officer for the Church Mission Society in the UK. Since ordination he has served in parishes, hospitals and a hospice; tutored in adult spiritual formation and served as editor for *ENGAGE* (formerly *Nota Bene* for STL/Wesley Owen). He is currently tutor for the Diocese of Carlisle, part-time school teacher and chaplain to Centerparcs.

Anton is married to Sue, a nurse with Hospice at Home and his inspiration.

Michael Lofthouse has over 40 years of management and leadership experience. He was a chief superintendent in the Kent Police, the deputy director of the Business School of Canterbury Christ Church University in Canterbury Diocese, and latterly as the director of LM Consultancy he provides advice and guidance to charitable and non-profit organizations. He has lectured at universities throughout the world in countries as diverse as China, Egypt and the USA. He is a visiting lecturer for the Department of International Security and Resilience at Cranfield University.

A word from the Chair of MODEM on *101 Great Ideas for Growing Healthy Churches*

ELIZABETH WELCH

101 Great Ideas marks a development from MODEM's previous books on leadership and management in that it offers short and focused pieces that will be easily accessible for a quick look in the face of particular issues that come up in a church's life.

It has a great wealth and variety of contributors. Some write from their 'hands on' experience of grappling with leadership issues within the church over many years. Others are regional and national church leaders. Some have extensive academic experience in writing and speaking on leadership and management, both in Britain and internationally. Others have a background in business or the voluntary sector. One of the advantages of this book is that the contributors represent a range of different Christian traditions. This brings about a mix of different approaches and a variety of insights which can be helpful across a spectrum of different situations.

Approaches to leadership and management in the churches arise out of a variety of different theological perspectives, balancing between more personal and more conciliar approaches. Each approach is shaped by a deep sense of the Trinitarian God who calls us into being and, in Christ, calls us to share in the work of his kingdom in the world. Attentiveness to God's world and the insights gained from a wide range of thinking about the way in which organizations are shaped and developed, is also helpful in shaping the present-day organizational realities of church life.

Undergirding this lies an openness to the Holy Spirit and a willingness to be led in new directions, building on the way in which the Spirit has led God's people over many centuries. Churches have not always modelled best practice in terms of either attentiveness to the Spirit or to the human needs and concerns revealed in different generations. This book is a contribution to the development of healthy churches. It offers snapshots of good practice and a range of thoughts and practical suggestions to aid the Christian people in a local community to develop and grow their life.

The Church in Western Europe has seen many challenges in the post-Enlightenment period. The social and philosophical emphasis on human autonomy, with the rise of the focus on the individual, has led to a diminishment of the authority of many traditional institutions. The positive aspect of this has been a greater sense of personal freedom and a growing challenge to corrupt and abusive practices within any institution. At the same time, this has brought about a challenge to traditional patterns of organizational life and a diminishment of the sense of shared responsibility. Women and men involved in leadership and management need to wrestle more vigorously with both the external pressures on an organization and the internal practices which help the organization to be healthy and to grow. This book offers snippets of support to help leaders and managers to be more visionary and effective.

I am grateful to the three editors of this book, John Nelson, Anton Müller and Michael Lofthouse, for the time, effort and creative energy they have put into bringing this book into being. MODEM as an organization is committed to developing new thinking in the areas of leadership and management and to drawing together networks of practitioners who are seeking to share insights as part of a learning community.

I pray that this book will offer a contribution to the ferment of ideas and practices that abound with regard to leadership and management, in a way that offers practical application in the setting of the local church, helping churches to be healthy and faith-filled organizations, to the glory of God.

Introduction to *101 Great Ideas for Growing Healthy Churches*

JOHN NELSON

Perhaps it is an age thing. I remember the days when you could lift a car bonnet and see the engine. You could access the nuts and bolts, clean the distributor cap, change the water pump, those things that made up the heart of the car and made it go. With the help of a good maintenance manual you could get stuck in and fix it. Today I lift the bonnet and all I see is a sheet of moulded plastic and a port for somebody else to plug in a computer. Only experts can now fix it!

I sometimes think this is what we have done to leadership and management in the Church. It has been encased in a sheet of expert moulded plastic. What should be a practical and accessible job has been made so complex that it is almost impossible for us to get our management hands dirty. Experts reign and there are not too many easy to follow manuals out there to encourage you not to rely on others; to help you get beneath the plastic; to help you get your management hands dirty.

This book is your church leadership and management manual. Like a good car manual you will be able access the book to give you ideas and instructions on how to start to engage and use those management spanners. Arranged alphabetically this is not bed-time reading but a manual that you can refer to at any time. After all, if you have a problem with the suspension you do not need to be wading through pages and pages dealing with the fuel injection system. And like a good car manual each topic is written by a proven practitioner; somebody who has had to fix it and make it work. An eclectic mix of instructions, case studies, quotes and diagnostic exercises all selected to help you to engage and address that leadership or management issue.

Most contributions are supported by a Bible reference offered by the author or suggested by the editorial team. The editorial team also selected a Top Tip drawn from or inferred by the topic under discussion. Alongside contributions the editorial team have placed a Business Perspective. It is important to note that these represent part of the editorial process in an attempt to bring an equivalent secular context into consideration.

At the heart of this book are the many contributions which aim to deal with the how and why of church management and leadership. Finally there is a self-reflective diagnostic exercise. Like all good manuals it can be read and shared by others in your team: designed for you to be able to pull off the shelf when required and presented concisely to allow you quickly to apply that management spanner. No moulded plastic formed of management jargon, no port for somebody else to fix. This is a practical manual to help you engage.

I am grateful to all those practitioners who contributed and to Michael Lofthouse and Anton Müller who have so expertly edited the book.

A Spiritual Reflection on *101 Great Ideas for Growing Healthy Churches*

ANTON MÜLLER

All of us, in whatever walk of life, need to be able to manage. Often we may hear someone say to another 'How are you managing?' Rarely do we hear the answer.

During my time as the spiritual care co-ordinator for a hospice I learned that enabling people to manage their terminal or life-limiting illness was something which required much more than the administering of pain-relieving drugs. In the face of terminal or long-term illness what was needed for each patient was an internal strategy for facing and coping with the world that was not only changing dramatically but seemed to be moving on without them. Of some patients it would be said, 'they have turned their face to the wall'.

Once in that frame of mind it was very hard to enable a patient to turn back and proceed with their journey through the world. Unless there is a strategy for facing this most important of journeys then to turn and face the wall is often the only option.

It is fundamental to our Christian theology that the fullness of life takes us through the journey of death. It cannot be avoided or ignored. The purpose of administering pain-relieving drugs in modern hospice care is to give each patient the opportunity to live until they die. To live life in all its fullness, with dignity and with quality.

Too often I see churches that have turned their faces to the wall and have cut themselves off from the world. They are stuck on the pain-relieving drugs of the past. They look to their past glories and past achievements rather than looking where they are in the now and where they are called to go in the future.

All churches have a past, a present and a future. For some that future may mean a closure, an ending, a death, while for others it may mean living in a new way. This is the way ahead for every church. Both scenarios require careful management and a strategy for dealing with the different kinds of closures ahead. Both scenarios have the possibilities for a new way of being.

If this were not so for a church then that church has not been living its life according to the theology which underpins our Christian faith. I recently heard about how the closure of one struggling church gave new life and growth to other churches around it. The death of one church gave new hope and being for the remnant of that church who found new life and ministry in the way forward. That church is growing.

A healthy church is one that understands that its life is based upon God's greatest idea – that of death and resurrection.

Every contribution in this book is a pointer to living a forward-thinking life. There are no contributions that talk about maintaining the status quo. Every contribution is offered as a strategy for managing the abundance of life to which God is calling every Christian and every church.

Given the opportunity to write a short quote of my own, it would be this: 'Managing the status quo of the church is called juggling. Managing the forward movement of the church is called strategy.'

I have no doubt that Jesus could have juggled if he wanted to, but instead he chose to stretch out his arms in a loving embrace that brings life and new ways of living and being.

I share with my editorial colleagues a great sense of the privilege that we have experienced in compiling these *101 Great Ideas*. We are privileged now to share these with you as you seek to build your own strategy for embracing the world as whole and healthy churches.

A Business Perspective on *101 Great Ideas for Growing Healthy Churches*

MICHAEL LOFTHOUSE

Get ready or go under! Those leading and managing a church now work in an environment that is dominated by secularism, where the authority of religion and religious organizations is declining. A destructive and threatening marketplace exists in which potential customers switch their allegiance to rival providers and where effective leadership and management is not an option, it is a necessity.

This competitive environment creates customer mobility and the related pressure that congregations are now consumers. It is becoming increasingly difficult to maintain or grow the customer base. This places on clergy added marketplace pressures regarding the content and structure of their religious services and organizations. Is the environment inviting? Are their products attractive? Is this what customers are prepared to 'buy'?

Leading and managing a church now also brings with it added challenging personal contemporary secular job demands. These pressures can lead to role conflict, isolation and a lack of professional autonomy. Ministry alone cannot guarantee a successful church. As secularization tightens its grip, religious organizations typically respond by attempting to replicate secular management, structures, practices and strategies, often with little understanding of consequences. They often fail to adequately prepare those who are to operationalize this 'new way' of working.

In today's church clergy must lead and manage with diminished institutional and personal legitimacy, while simultaneously dealing with a work context characterized by high expectations and congregational change, often without the necessary leadership and management skills and competencies.

That is the bad news. The good news is that it is possible and many have thrived and prospered in this challenging environment; which has meant that their churches and congregations have thrived and prospered. This book is a testament to this assertion.

What do I recommend to meet these challenges? I have a simple prescription. Adopt an internal personal and organizational orientation towards good leadership and management practices; learn from successful competitors and peers, including those from the secular world; be prepared to get your leadership and management hands dirty, be adaptable, adventurist and honest, especially with yourself and be prepared to fail; find and refine your own leadership and management style; and, importantly, accept that ministry alone is no longer sufficient to sustain your church.

Remember, there is only one measure of effective church leadership and management and that is a profitable church.

Great Idea 1

Agree a Vision

JAMES NEWCOME

> I tell you that if two of you on earth agree about anything you ask for, it will be done for you by my Father in heaven
> Matthew 18.19
>
> **Top Tip:** Listen hard before saying too much.
>
> **Business Perspective:** The successful organization understands the necessity for creating a vision as it becomes the unifying force for the organization. Without a vision an organization creates a disparate set of individuals who all like to pursue their own agendas.

Agreeing a vision is one of the most important things any church leader can do. It contributes directly to the growth of a healthy church. Consider these three key questions:

With whom should you agree?

Any vision needs to be agreed with:

God	The vision should be his.
A leadership team	The vision should be 'ours', not just 'mine'.
The congregation	Not everyone will agree, but all should be involved in the process.

1

Why should you agree?

Agreeing the vision with God, a leadership team and the congregation is essential because if the vision and its timing does not come from God it is unlikely to get very far. If the process isn't shared and worked on by other leaders there is a real danger of missing the point as well as alienating vital colleagues. If people don't 'own' the vision they simply won't follow where you try to lead.

How can you agree a vision?

No vision gets wholehearted agreement without a careful and sometimes lengthy process of preparation. This involves:

- Locating areas of dissatisfaction in the life of the church. This could be anything from uncomfortable pews to lack of local outreach. Listening carefully to people's hopes, fears and longings as well as their deepest frustrations provides a starting point for discussion as well as an initial source of energy.
- Holding evenings and perhaps whole days of prayer for listening to God. These could sometimes be accompanied by fasting. They should always include written feedback.
- Working with a small group at articulating a clear picture of 'where we want to go'. The picture needs to be realistic about the current situation as well as specific about the 'preferred future'.
- Identifying individuals and groups who may be opposed to the developing vision. Some may be complacent about the status quo and averse to change of any kind. Others might not understand or they might misunderstand what is going on. Others still might feel threatened by the direction in which they sense the church is heading. It matters that leaders should spend time with these people, listening to their concerns and explaining what is going on and why.

- Gathering all necessary information. For example, if the vision includes a building project the leaders will need to know what it will cost in time and effort as well as money.
- Creating a plan of action or strategy so that when the vision is finally presented people will know when they will start and how they can get from where they currently are to where they are going.
- Clarifying the roles and responsibilities of those who will lead and manage the change.
- Living the vision with infectious enthusiasm so that others will be drawn in and want to share what excites and motivates you.

The overall aim of this whole process of preparation is that when the right moment comes to present the vision formally, people will say not just 'I know what you mean' but rather 'how can I be involved?'

For reflection and discussion

1 What is the current vision for your church?
2 What areas of church life should be developed or dropped in order to fulfil the vision?
3 What opportunities are there ahead which will enable the spiritual growth of your church?
4 What obstacles need to be considered and understood before articulating your vision to the wider community of the church?

Great Idea 2

Ask the Lord his Business

JOHN ADAIR

All leaders worthy of the name grow their businesses. The first question you have to ask yourself is what business are we in?

The business of the Church is the business of Jesus, 'my Father's business', namely the coming of the kingdom of God on earth.

A healthy church is a community of purpose. It looks upwards and outwards, constrained only by the highest inner personal necessity, which is to love.

All healthy churches have a shared aspect. They all have that unmistakable Christian hallmark of humility. Like their individual members they simply and continually ask: 'Lord, what will you have me to do?'

Great Idea 4

Avoid Judging other People

JOHN DEVINE

Try to say 'Yes' to people rather than 'No'. The Spirit speaks to us through the most unlikely people and in the most unlikely places. Never imagine that the institutional Church has a monopoly on the Spirit – the Spirit actively subverts any attempt at control. Avoid judging other people. It is usually the prelude to similar mistakes in your own life. But don't be afraid when you make a mess of things either. My personal sinfulness is sometimes the only way that God can get through to me.

Great Idea 5

Be a Listening Church

PATRICK GOH

> You are worried about many things, but only one thing is needed
> Luke 10.41–42
>
> **Top Tip:** Be ready to lay down your own agenda and really listen.
>
> **Business Perspective:** A successful organization understands that profitability rests in the full and active participation of its members. Consequently active leaders develop an active listening organization.

During a retreat at a Franciscan friary where the theme was leadership and diversity the Abbot was asked whether he had any tips on how to honour diversity at a practical level. He replied:

> If you believe that God works through all of us, you need to somehow enact this belief. One way of doing this is to enter into any conversation with a spirit of anticipation, expecting to hear how God is working through people and what God is saying to them.

On the whole, we don't do this well. Instead, our conversations are more often about telling others what we feel God is saying to us. In a leadership context, this can lead to an overly top down approach to decision making.

To address this, my colleagues and I have developed a tool called the 'keynote listener'. This is based on the concept of honouring the voices of the community and the importance of listening in agreeing a common vision. This is a conversational tool that reverses the normal communication process by asking people in authority not to present what they know and think, but to listen for the wisdom of others. It is an attempt to gather the collective wisdom of the whole community (church).

We have used this methodology for church events such as visioning meetings, annual church meetings and youth conferences. It works best when it is possible to bring the whole system, or as many as possible, into one place. Rather than having the usual sermons from 'keynote speakers', we reframe them as 'keynote listeners', whose role is to listen carefully to the ideas of participants throughout the day.

The idea is to structure enquiry sessions on the main issue we are addressing in creative ways, for example, using talk, posters, drama, music, dance, etc. The role of keynote listeners is to attend these sessions, listen carefully to the contributions, feedback and questions.

The keynote listeners are asked to listen out for:

- Ideas, thoughts, and opinions
- Common themes and shared concerns
- Genuine differences
- Motivating values
- Concerns and worries
- Passion and feeling
- Visions and ideals
- All the forms of communication, both verbal and non-verbal
- Content, passion, and perspective.

There are a number of important principles for the keynote listener:

1 Try not to influence the conversations but remain in silent listening mode.
2 Set your own thoughts and opinions aside and listen openly.

3 Listen with curiosity and fascination, even when you hear ideas with which you may not personally agree.
4 Enter the 'grammar' of the participants and hear the way they express their ideas. Hear their words and how they connect ideas and thought.
5 See how participants relate to and interact with one another.
6 Stay faithful to your role and remember that this is not a time for you to put forth your thoughts, but a moment in which you can concentrate on the ideas of others.

Keynote listeners are then given the opportunity to reflect on what they have heard and to share their insights in a structured feedback session. This often works well as a conversation rather than someone simply talking from the front. The following are useful questions for this session:

- What surprised you in what you heard?
- What moved you?
- What most intrigued you?
- What were the hotspots?
- Did you have a sense of what was unsaid?
- Were there elephants in the room?
- What is different for you now after being a keynote listener?
- What would you like to learn more about?
- What would you say is the 'voice' of this community?
- What differences still divide this community based on what you heard?
- What is one piece of wisdom you gained today?
- What are the major themes you have heard?
- What new insights did you learn?

The purpose of this exercise is to help change the culture of your church from top down to relational leadership, where leadership is about helping your community make sense of complexity, and suggest ways of moving forward together.

For reflection and discussion

If we have been listening ...

1 What are the children and young people saying?
2 What are the families/singles in our church and community saying?
3 What are the elderly in our church and community saying?
4 If the way we do things in our church is the result of listening to others in our church and community, what have they been saying?

Great Idea 6

Be Able to Say Sorry

ANTON MÜLLER

> Whoever is forgiven much loves much
> Luke 7.47
>
> **Top Tip:** Love means always being able to say sorry.
>
> **Business Perspective:** Successful organizations understand that a creative and profitable organization accepts that mistakes will be part of its operational life. They understand that mistakes are based on the belief that if the organization had done something different it would have been more successful. This enables them to learn from the mistake, correct it, become more profitable, rather than waste energy on blame.

When a business has been caught out it is likely that they will engage in a strategic apology which more often than not means 'I'm sorry I was caught', or 'I'm sorry that you are offended', rather than being sorry for the misdoing or for causing the offence.

The reason for such strategic apologies is nearly always about saving face or saving one's job. This, however, is not apology as Christians should understand it.

Christian confession and apology can only take place in the context of forgiveness. When we apologize for something we are also asking for forgiveness. An apology that is not seeking forgiveness is not an apology, it is a political manoeuvre.

Jesus apologizes for the human race when he says, 'Father forgive them for they know not what they do.' As a church we can apologize for the shortcomings of our race and we can seek God's forgiveness for the whole of the human race. This is what Jesus does and we can do the same because by his death and resurrection we have been made like him.

What are the leadership implications for the Church and for the world?

There must be a culture of forgiveness in the organization that must come from the leadership of the organization. This is called a 'no-blame culture' and in such a culture all members of the organization are safe and free to apologize. Vital to this process is an acceptance of responsibility at all levels. Acceptance of responsibility also means an acceptance of consequence. A no-blame culture requires more of every member of the organization not less, hence the need for compassionate forgiveness. A no-blame culture is more creative and consequently more productive. It is not a free-for-all or a disregard for the vision of the organization. There is an acceptance that mistakes will be made on the way to success.

A blame culture is often a risk-averse organization that stifles participation, creativity and productivity which is the engine of profitability.

Consider the parable of the unforgiving servant. In this story the master, the leader of the business, sets the precedent for a culture of forgiveness but the ungrateful servant fails to live according to that precedent.

God has set the business and organization of his Church within a culture of forgiveness. Confession and repentance can only take place within such a culture. Confession and repentance will not take place within a culture of judgement and condemnation. The world judges and condemns and litigation suits lurk behind every potential mishap. In such a world apology and forgiveness are dismissed as weakness while that world is becoming increasingly sick and disabled by judgement and condemnation.

A culture of apology and forgiveness are the strengths of an organization, not its weakness. Those who have the courage to apologize, to forgive and to be forgiven show true strength and true leadership wherever they are in the organization. In biblical terms they are the ones who will be vindicated, healed and made whole.

Too often it seems that the story of the prodigal son is one which the Church likes to tell but seldom wants to live. The older brother of that story is alive and well in many parts of the Church today, both lay and ordained, at all levels.

The lesson of the prodigal son in the end is not a lesson about repentance, it is a lesson about unconditional love and acceptance 'even while we are still far off'.

For reflection and discussion

1 What is the present culture of your church?
2 How did your church respond to the last occasion where mistakes were made?
3 When was the last time you accepted full responsibility for a mistake that you made and apologized?
4 How will you create a no-blame culture in your church?

Great Idea 7

Be About Your Father's Business – Part 1

MICHAEL LOFTHOUSE

> My Father is always at his work to this very day
> and I too am working
> John 5.17
>
> **Top Tip:** Church leaders need to formulate profitable objectives for their organization.
>
> **Business Perspective:** When leaders know clearly what their objectives are and can legitimate those decisions within the management team efficacy is the result. Effective leaders discover how their environment and the capability of their organization are changing by gathering facts through a continuous process of scanning, research, consultation and monitoring. Formulating objectives that are feasible, sustainable and acceptable is the primary task of the leader of any organization. This is the management heart of leadership. And why do leaders engage in this process? It is because they want their organization to grow, continue and succeed. They want it to be a profitable organization.

The Church is no different; it needs to grow, continue and succeed. It needs to be a profitable organization. Church leaders need to formulate profitable objectives for their organization.

The difficulty is that the collection, analysis and exchange of information uses resources, is time consuming and incurs costs, and the process is often outside the skill set of most church leaders. An additional significant difficulty is that church leaders conflate ministry with management. They fail to disaggregate the organization leading to aggregated decisions that are bounded by individual preference.

The first step is to understand and accept that at the management level the church is a business; that effective management is the necessary foundation of effective ministry. Now a church leader can disaggregate the organization so that strategic elements of the organization can be identified (see Figure 1). By disaggregating the organization we create a linear model that segments the organization into its component parts.

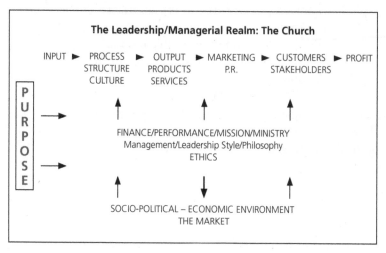

Figure 1

Now we can engage in a decision-making process that is also disaggregated as we make decisions within the confines of each component part of the organization. Given a problem or opportunity we can identify which part of the organization needs our managerial attention. For example, one of the organization's products, the Sunday service, is failing to attract a target audience as defined within our purpose, and as a consequence we fail to be in profit in this area of our ministry.

By utilizing the disaggregated business model we can examine in detail each component part of the organization to find a solution. Perhaps the problem is in the marketing, or in the product; it is just not attractive to the target audience, or in the economic environment; we have failed to invest in the infrastructure surrounding the product.

This disaggregated business model also draws our attention to the connective nature of our business. The efficacy of each component part of the organization is reliant on the efficacy of the rest of the component parts. For example, a church could be delivering excellent ministry to a dwindling set of customers. Perhaps the problem is in leadership or finance, we simply do not have enough capital to expand or support the infrastructure of the church. Perhaps the problem is the current culture of the organization?

The challenge is that you must be able not only to disaggregate the organization, to think of it as a business, you also have to take the next step and disaggregate each of the component parts of the business.

The tough question to ask is: 'What counts as profit for your church?' You have to be able to disaggregate profit by creating performance targets that are connected to your purpose. And of course this means disaggregating your purpose.

For reflection and discussion

1 How do you measure profit in your church?
2 Are your meetings dominated by discourses that are generalized and aggregated?
3 Is it difficult to reach implementable management interventions that support your purpose and generate profit?
4 Are you managerially frustrated? Why?

Great Idea 8

Be About Your Father's Business – Part 2

PHILIP DOWN

Who then is the faithful and prudent manager? Blessed is that slave whom his master will find at work when he arrives. Truly I tell you he will put that one in charge of all his possessions
Luke 12.42–44

Top Tip: It is necessary to improve the disaggregation of every element of the organization's life until you can see the issues clearly enough for either celebration or reform.

Business Perspective: Successful organizations understand that they are first and foremost a business where profit and loss is equivalent to life or death.

In the business and commercial world a production model disaggregates the various complex steps into more fundamental elements for measurement, refinement and development. This enables the manager to understand successes, to treat failures and to overcome risks.

How might the church, as an organization interested in producing certain outcomes, be able to disaggregate the elements of its own organizational life into more recognizable fundamental elements?

It might just help church leaders manage change better and be more productive in their common life with respect to desired outcomes (see Figure 2).

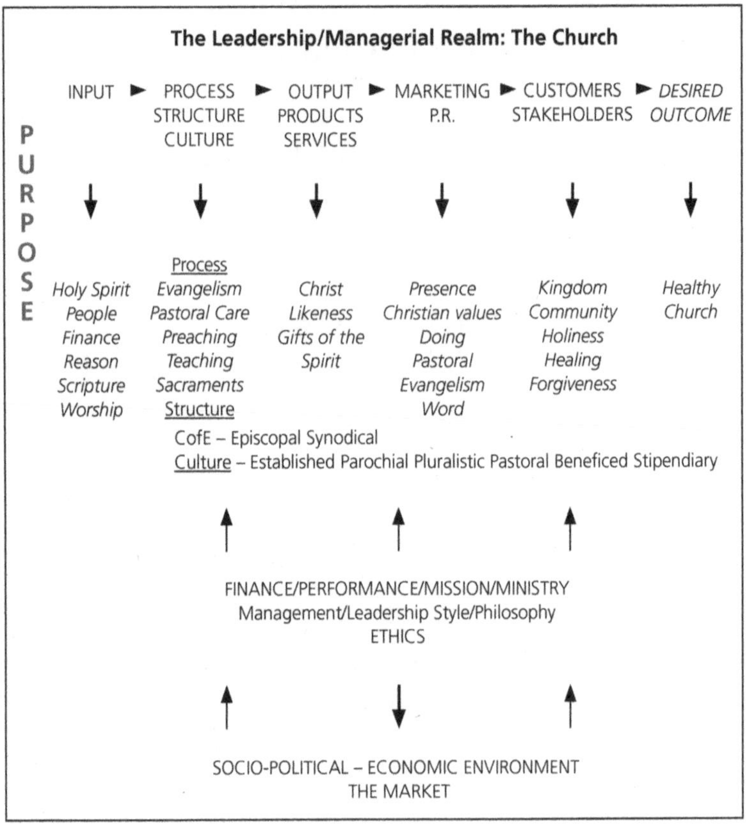
The Leadership/Managerial Realm: The Church
INPUT
PROCESS STRUCTURE CULTURE
OUTPUT PRODUCTS SERVICES
MARKETING P.R.
CUSTOMERS STAKEHOLDERS
DESIRED OUTCOME
PURPOSE
Holy Spirit People Finance Reason Scripture Worship
Process Evangelism Pastoral Care Preaching Teaching Sacraments Structure
Christ Likeness Gifts of the Spirit
Presence Christian values Doing Pastoral Evangelism Word
Kingdom Community Holiness Healing Forgiveness
Healthy Church
CofE – Episcopal Synodical
Culture – Established Parochial Pluralistic Pastoral Beneficed Stipendiary
FINANCE/PERFORMANCE/MISSION/MINISTRY
Management/Leadership Style/Philosophy
ETHICS
SOCIO-POLITICAL – ECONOMIC ENVIRONMENT
THE MARKET

Figure 2

Under the scrutiny of disaggregation we are faced with a number of challenges by such a materialist model.

In the commercial world it is relatively simple to work backwards through the linear model from the desired outcome to establish what is required in the other parts of the organization. For example, how many widgets need to be produced and how, for which customer and in what time frame to produce a profit?

This is not so simple for the church leader as we tend not to be driven by the concept of profit. Instead of talking about profit we can talk about a fruitful and productive church where we find that 'ministry' is a desired outcome while simultaneously being an input, a process, an output and the key to the market!

Therefore in terms of disaggregation we need a deeper level of understanding in respect of each part of the model. Consequently ministry as an 'input' might be the conduct of a wedding or some other occasional office.

Ministry as an output might be the married couple not only being married but being cared for pastorally by the church. Ministry as a process would be the actions by which such care has been shown to the couple by the church.

Ministry as a marketing operation would be the marriage leaflets produced by the church which describe such care, although the act of showing such care is perhaps the strongest sales pitch to the market and is to do with relationship. The desired outcome is 'ministry' as a relationship fulfilled in marriage and supported by the church both as agent and caring friend.

It is necessary to improve the disaggregation of every element of the organization's life until you can see the issues clearly enough for either celebration or reform.

Perhaps our best advantage in reflecting on the life of the church in this way is to be reminded constantly of the purpose(s) of the church by which the remainder of the model must be judged and, where necessary, reformed. Conformity to purpose will drive the engine of production in all its parts. Purpose gives energy!

Such purpose needs to include: the worship of God, and the love of neighbour.

The church, in today's world, has great challenges in the areas of 'process', 'outputs' and 'marketing'. This is the world where fresh expressions of church may be able to help and where more traditional elements will have a place but may need to be reformed. It is here that a disaggregated management model will help.

Ultimately the Spirit of God will use the faith and practice of the church as God needs but there is an abiding task for the disciples of Jesus and the family of Christ and that is to be mindful of the life of the Spirit and the calling of God. That life and calling usually involves sacrifice and change for the purposes of healing a broken world. It cannot make sense merely as self-serving religion.

For reflection and discussion

1 How would you further disaggregate things such as 'mission', 'pastoral care', 'evangelism' and 'prayer' expressed as outputs in the life of your church?
2 Try to disaggregate 'ministry' further; as 'input', 'process' and 'output'.
3 Who are your customers in your local community and how does the process relate to them?
4 How many of the 'desired outcomes' (profit in the business sense) of your church are of benefit to the stakeholder groups you can identify in your community? If they do not bring a benefit, why not? What needs to change in the columns to the left of the 'customers' to improve this situation?

Great Idea 9

Be an Agent for Change

MICHAEL LOFTHOUSE

> You are the salt of the earth
> Matthew 5.13
>
> **Top Tip:** Openly encourage change.
>
> **Business Perspective:** Successful organizations understand that innovation and change is their natural state.

Anyone who has an itch to make a difference in their local church can be an agent for change. No matter whether old or young, lay or ordained. Consequently leaders and managers of their churches must be vigilant to uncover and encourage those with the itch. They must also be humble enough to recognize that they are not solely in charge of change.

Church people seem to like stability. The reality is that if constant change is not happening in your church it is standing still or worse, dying, or dead.

This is not to underestimate the leadership and managerial difficulty of change. It is a challenging and frustrating process.

Most churches change and grow through a series of changes suggested by people throughout the congregation. This process often happens outside the formal structure of the church. Consequently these changes while important are not maximized profitably. It is important that the leadership of the church recognizes who is driving the change so that it can be nurtured and directed to fulfil the mission of the church.

Such change happens through a balance of good pastoral care and openness to a range of new ideas emerging sometimes from unlikely places within the church.

It will come as a surprise to many that the church has to change and adapt in just the same way as all other organizations. One of the best ways to see that God's Spirit is moving in a congregation is to see how much adaptation has been made over the last five years. Another measure is to look at how many people have joined and to ask them why.

Too often clergy think that they are structurally bound to lead all change and they become frustrated when people do not respond well to their ideas. The secret is to gain the agreement of key people and groups and to make sure that everyone knows what is expected of them to drive the change into something profitable for the church. It is important to check progress at agreed times on the journey of change. Always celebrate success publicly, thank those who have profitably contributed while evaluating and learning from your mistakes. The process of change inevitably involves both.

Change agents can often be viewed by the leadership as 'the awkward squad', always complaining or disagreeing. Successful leaders recognize that all church members are potentially change agents.

A church committed to continual change is like a ship that has left the safety of the harbour and which has to navigate a way across the open seas to new destinations. The crew has to trust their captain and be willing to use their skills to get to the new place. The crew will be encouraged and willing to put in new ideas to make the voyage exciting with actions as well as with words. Too many churches are like ships seemingly stuck in dry dock waiting for something to happen. The reality is, they are never going to sail, and if they put to sea, they will inevitably sink.

For reflection and discussion

1 How is change understood in your church?
2 When did you last stifle a change initiative and why?
3 Who is responsible for change in your church?
4 What suggestions for change are you prepared to revisit?

Great Idea 10

Be Discontented!

KEITH LAMDIN

There are three essentials for every leader – discontent, vision and courage – all shaped by discipleship of the risen Christ and a passion for God's kingdom.

Great Idea 11

Be Friendly with Science
and Medicine

DAVID TAYLOR

> You created my inmost being, you knit me together in my mother's womb. I praise you because I am fearfully and wonderfully made; your works are wonderful,
> I know that full well
> Psalm 139.13–14
>
> **Top Tip:** Science should be regarded as a way of trying to come to terms with the world around us.
>
> **Business Perspective:** Successful commercial organizations understand that customers live in many different worlds. Their product range takes account of the different experiences and needs generated by these worlds. No successful business would deny the existence of another world but would attempt to engage with it in order to increase profitability.

There are practical and theological reasons why we should be friendly with science and medicine. On a practical level we need to embrace science and medicine because they are part of the world in which we live. This is also the theological reason!

It is easy to see science as a threat, and faith as an irrational response to a rational world. In practice science is simply a way of explaining the rational. Most scientists would probably qualify that by saying that science is a way of trying to measure and understand things, as best we can, given what we already know. Very few scientific facts can be relied on as being absolute truths, but most will be reasonably good approximations to reality. So science should simply be regarded as a way of trying to come to terms with the world around us.

There is a tendency to try to polarize the arguments, by stating that science and faith do different things, and on the one hand that is self-evidently true. However, it is a mistake to think that neither has anything to say to the other.

Science can give us a much greater and detailed picture of the wonders of creation, and faith can respond to that with awe and delight. Faith, in turn, can show that some of the wonders cannot be measured in metres or kilograms but that the human response is actually part of the understanding.

The full picture only comes into focus when the two perspectives are aligned. We know so much about the creation of the cosmos which is exciting, as is the fact that there is so much more to learn about it. Without an understanding of the human place in the cosmos we would miss the full picture and risk damaging it irrevocably.

Christian understanding of the place of humans in the cosmos is shaped by what we find in scripture and through faith in Jesus.

There is a second reason why we should befriend science and medicine. That is because, as science and technology advance, we need to be able to help people think through the implications of the possible. This could be by asking challenging and thought-provoking questions regarding ethics, or by pointing out the possibility of unintended consequences. Of course, people of other faiths or none can and do raise ethical questions and point out moral dilemmas, but we have undeniable insights into what it means to be a person.

We can offer a really valuable service to a scientist or a clinician if we can sit and actually listen to the things that concern them. It often helps to have some understanding of the underlying science, because then the conversation is more informed. But it is also good if we just provide a listening ear for those with a burden and allow them to talk themselves through a problem.

In a perfect world, the relationship between science, medicine and the Christian faith would be a conversation, each informing the other, bringing fresh perspectives and shaping each others' values and understanding.

That can only happen if we befriend science and medicine.

For reflection and discussion

1 How do you take time to celebrate the gifts we have been given through scientific and medical progress?
2 How do you keep yourself informed about scientific, medical and technological advancements?
3 What are the ethical and moral dilemmas raised by scientific, medical and technological advancements?
4 How will you encourage your congregation to engage these dilemmas?

Great Idea 12

Be Inclusive, not Divisive

JOE RILEY

Be inclusive, not divisive, in expanding Christian fellowship. Learn from history. Expect and accept further truths and revelations; there will be many. Befriend science and medicine, which are also gifts. Put people before buildings and set community before self. If ever in doubt ask, 'What would Jesus do?'

Great Idea 13

Be 'In-house' and 'Out-house'!

JOHN NELSON

May the words of my mouth and the meditation of my heart
be pleasing in your sight
Psalm 19.14

Top Tip: Be the best in the diocese and equal to the best in the
community.

Business Perspective: Successful organizations realize that
reputation can be lost quickly through poor publicity. Control
of your media output in a dynamic environment is an essential
business requirement. No successful organization fails to have its
own in-house publication whose message is directed externally.

The parish magazine was much the same as any other, it was
monthly, A5, 25 pages, black and white, £5 a year with com-
plimentary copies delivered to every household in the parish at
Christmas and Easter. And like so many magazines ... there was
no editor!

What follows are ten lessons to get your magazine up and running as a vital part of the church's mission and outreach.

1 Fully support your magazine editor

The editor had just resigned for the same reason as the previous
editor. They both felt their role and work was undervalued. They

had both spent sleepless nights worried sick about the blank pages left to fill! Mission and outreach through the magazine needs a team approach supported by the church.

2 Be church and parish related

Despite the title 'parish magazine', it wasn't a 'parish' magazine at all. It was a 'church members' magazine full of reports from church and church-related meetings and not much else.

The parish magazine must appeal to all members of the parish, churchgoers and non-churchgoers alike. It must make them aware of the church, its message and pastoral role as well as information about the parish and its people. Be 'in-house' but be also 'out-house'.

The parish magazine can show how successfully the life of the church connects with the life of the parish – or not!

3 Meet monthly as a team – plan, share the load, enjoy!

This means that your communications committee is likely to be the hardest-working sub-committee of the PCC! The team must work hard to report on and publicize events, provide information about the church, its services and activities, that will have meaning and impact for the church AND the parish. Think ahead, lay out the year ahead and plan accordingly. There are only twelve magazines! You can do this.

4 Draw upon the talents and experience of your church members and build your team strategically

What is needed is an editor and deputy, a distributor/co-ordinator, writers and illustrators, graphic designers and someone getting adverts. In this case they were found, but you have to go out and find them. You will be amazed at the talents available to you in your church.

5 Dare to be different ... go glossy

An attractive cover attracts readers. Invest in a professionally designed cover. One of the church members in this case was a former graphic designer and a partnership was formed with a local printing firm to have the cover professionally printed. It was worth it.

6 Be businesslike, cover costs ... make a profit!

Should the church magazine have a cover price? Whatever decision is made, the magazine should cover its costs. Advertising is the obvious way to cover most or all of the costs and has the added value of not only being a local resource for events, goods and services but there is an outreach value in seeking advertising income from local businesses.

7 Review the market – is your magazine getting out there?

Every church and electoral roll member should receive a copy of the magazine, but also every business, hotel, pub, hospital, surgery, dental, bus and rail waiting room in your parish. Some of these venues may well be some of your leading subscribers.

8 Don't stay local ... go global

Readers of the parish magazine should be stimulated to see the wider picture: to be helped to see their local church in the global context; to be helped to interpret world events through the eyes of the Christian faith.

Contributions from those able to reflect spiritually and theologically on world events are an important part any parish magazine. Such contributors should have the ability to interpret world events and to challenge conventional wisdom in a constructive way that opens up real thinking and dialogue between church and community. Choose your contributors wisely.

9 Be the best you can be

With the resources now available to so many people there is no excuse for poorly produced material. Strive to ensure that your magazine is regarded not only as the best in the diocese but comparable to other publications in the community. It will prove to be a very important and powerful form of outreach in the parish and local community.

10 It's mission, so pray

If the vision for the parish magazine is one of mission and outreach for the kingdom of God, then that work cannot prosper unless underpinned, daily, by prayer. The editorial team should meet to pray and the church should remember the editorial team in prayer. Pray that doors will open to the parish magazine along with the hearts and minds of those who read it.

For reflection and discussion

1 Is your magazine in-house or out-house?
2 Is your magazine both a mouthpiece for the church and a forum for the parish?
3 Is your magazine editor supported by people and prayer?
4 Does your magazine stand out from other organizations' magazines?

Great Idea 14

Be in the Business of Making Disciples

MIKE BREEN

Go into all the world and make disciples of all nations
Matthew 28.19

Top Tip: If you 'make' disciples, you will always get the church. But if you're seeking to build the church, you rarely get disciples.

Business Perspective: In the commercial world successful commercial businesses put sustained effort into creating and nurturing advocates for their brand. Advocates both inside and outside the organization practically and verbally support the organization by buying, using and recommending the product to others. In commercial terms external advocates are a very cost effective way of sustaining the business. They become emotionally attached to the organization.

The church also needs advocates.

In the church context, advocates are disciples. Discipleship may not sound new or revolutionary, but if taken seriously, it will change everything for you and your church and your community.

There is not a leadership problem in the Church in the West. There is not a missional problem. There is a discipleship problem. If we make disciples, like Jesus made disciples, the way we're supposed to, we get more leaders than we can handle and more vision and action for mission than we will have ever seen. The same can be seen in every successful commercial business.

That's the way Jesus did it.

That's the way his disciples did it.

That's the way the early church did it.

That's the way every missional movement in history has done it.

And yet there is a full-fledged discipleship crisis which has led to a full-fledged crisis in the Western Church. What we have failed to understand is that the church is the effect of discipleship rather than the cause. In other words, if you make disciples, you will always get the church. But if you're seeking to build the church, you rarely get disciples.

If you wish to make disciples there are two managerial questions that need to be answered.

1   What is your plan for making disciples?
2   Does the plan work?

Most of us are in communities that plan for making disciples, but sadly, these plans haven't really worked for quite some time. The absence of an effective discipleship plan is often a product of church-based focus.

The discipleship plan at St Thomas Sheffield works and is based on that vision which has ultimately spawned a global discipling and missional movement. We started something we call Huddle, which is a group of four to ten people who are being intentionally discipled by the Huddle leader which, while similar in size to a small group, is actually quite different. The Huddle meets at the very least, every two weeks.

The leaders invest in the disciples and the disciples give the leaders access to their life outside the Huddle space. At the end of every Huddle gathering, each person in the group will be able to answer two questions:

1   What is God saying to me right now?
2   In the next two weeks, what am I going to do about it?

The next time the Huddle gathers the leader will ask, 'Did you do what you said you were going to do?'

The purpose here is to inject accountability into the process. We cannot make disciples without intentionality and accountability. Jesus didn't.

It goes beyond this. Every person entering a Huddle knows that within 12 to 18 months they will start a Huddle of their own. Why? Because every disciple disciples.

That's not radical. That's not revolutionary, that's just the Great Commission.

For reflection and discussion

1 Do you have a discipleship plan?
2 Is the model outlined above practical in your church?
3 Do members of your congregation always act as advocates for the church?
4 What strategies do you have for countering a negative view of your church?

Great Idea 15

Believe that You too can Change the Church

MALCOLM GRUNDY

Here I am, send me
Isaiah 6.8

Top Tip: With the blessing of God's Spirit you too can be an instrument for change.

Business Perspective: Successful organizations understand that if their staff are emotionally attached to the organization they are more creative and productive.

Local churches are not what they used to be. They have learned to adapt and change with great skill. One reason for this is that God will not let them stand still. Churchgoing as a social convention has died. Most people go to church nowadays because they want to. Many congregations are made up of people who have come from a number of other denominations. This can bring riches of faith and ideas; it can also bring tensions about the ways change can be brought in.

There are many people who do wonder why they should still keep going to church. They leave worship more frustrated than inspired and equipped to face another week. Church life and worship can be stuck in the past. For many people faith is too precious to be trapped in this way. People of faith have more hope than despair.

The Holy Spirit brings new life and resurrection wherever there is openness to change. Churches are renewed by Spirit-filled and Spirit-disturbed people! God is also at work bringing change and new life outside the church all over the world. Many ideas from the rest of life can be put to good use inside the church. This is because the best ideas do not belong to any one race or nation: they are about love and forgiveness, reconciliation and justice.

Jesus was very disturbed by what he saw in the religion of his day. He challenged those in authority and overturned the tables of the moneychangers; a story told in each of the four gospels. He wanted God's houses to be places of prayer. Today Jesus wants people with vision to change the church and renew everyday life. People full of prayerful ideas are God's chosen people.

It is both comforting and distressing that we do not know what the church of the future will look like. It has changed, in every part of the world, more than we could ever have imagined over the past 50 years. Some changes have been on a large scale like the use of modern language in the liturgy and the renewal of church music. Many other changes have been begun by one person or one group having a good idea and wanting to try it out. Then the idea caught on and began something which snowballed into a big change.

With the blessing of God's Spirit you too can be an instrument for change. If you are inspired or just cannot let go of an idea that has come to you, it is possible that you are being prompted from somewhere to become an agent for change and to make a difference wherever God has called you to be.

For reflection and discussion

1 In managerial terms, what do you understand by the term 'change'?
2 What do you do to generate commitment to change in your church?
3 How do you see change as a principle of God's interaction with the world?
4 What is the level of your own commitment to change in your church?

Great Idea 17

Be the Church of God

CHARLES GORDON-LENNOX

Shortly after being elected to the Church Assembly in 1960 at the age of 30 I was invited to a conference on the laity by Bishop John Robinson, later author of *Honest to God*. It was the first time I had heard the phrase that has stayed with me ever since: 'The laity are not the helpers of the clergy so that the clergy can do their job, but the laity are the whole people of God so that they can be the Church.'

Great Idea 18

Be Mindful of Management

PETER RUDGE

> Let us make people in our image to be like ourselves.
> They will be master over all life
> Genesis 1.26

Top Tip: Learn from the history of management and choose wisely.

Business Perspective: Successful business managers understand that there is no single management style and that there is the opportunity to draw from a variety of management styles. They realize that there is a wealth of management knowledge to be discovered through historical and academic study which allows the manager to situationally select the most appropriate management approach.

The body of knowledge commonly known as management first appeared during the 800-year period following the time of St Thomas Aquinas, c 1226–74, a Dominican monk canonized in 1323, who argued that reason and faith were compatible. Its place in that phase is a way of indicating its character. The period was marked by a rebellion against or a rejection of theology or even an entire disregard of it.

One of the first to break the chain of the ties of scholasticism was Machiavelli in the field of politics. The next was Galileo in relation to astronomy; the contention between him and the Church is widely known; so is the instance of Darwin in the field of life sciences. Others grew up unnoticed by the Church such as Descartes in philosophy; so too were such subjects as economics, psychology and sociology. Alongside these was management.

It emerged as a sequel to the Industrial Revolution in the eighteenth century, though under the name of Onward Industry. Management writers Mooney and Reilly have traced the awareness of management to preceding centuries in the military and to preceding millennia to the building of the pyramids. It grew up without any reference to theology though the Church occasionally expressed reservations about the nature of the new society. Witness the hymn 'Jerusalem' and its reference to 'those dark satanic mills'; and there were the Tolpuddle Martyrs too.

Nor did the Church lay claim to management or to any of the other subjects that arose in this phase of history. The Roman Catholic Church in 1870 in the first Vatican Council echoed the voices of all the churches in defining its area of interest as 'matters of faith and morals'. That was all it had left from the time when theology was the queen of the sciences at the time of Aquinas. Since then its range has diminished to matters of sex and reproduction. Hence the Church of today has no claim to or interest in matters of management.

There was a further factor which closed out any interest in the subject. The view of management at the time of the Industrial Revolution became deeply ingrained in people's understanding, so much so that the prevailing view of management came to be called the classical form of management. Another title according to the social scientist Weber was the bureaucratic form; while a term such as mechanistic was also used to reveal even more clearly the precise nature of what was conceived as management.

This view of management became so ingrained in the unconscious memory of the whole population and not just the scholars that even the most removed from the field had absorbed its universal qualities and used this form of control without even recognizing its source or character.

Anybody who wanted to manage anything was innately equipped with a never-failing source of guidance that was in the Church also. Church leaders along with everyone else expressed in their actions this innate awareness of the way to go. Some who became aware of its harshness took up an alternative and opposite line through the human relations approach which is considered to be a much more humane way. But still the mechanistic view remained hidden, but often operative, in spite of the apparent gloss on the human relations side. It's no wonder that the Church has seen no need for any reliance on management. It was innately there.

For reflection and discussion

1 What is your understanding of the word management?
2 What value is there in exploring the range of management styles that have come down to us through history?
3 What aspects of management do you think could be of most benefit in growing healthy churches?
4 What aspects of management do you feel have no place in the church?

Great Idea 19

Be Personally Effective

MALCOLM GRUNDY

> If anyone sets his heart on being a leader, they desire a noble task
> 1 Timothy 3.1
>
> **Top Tip:** You can fool some of the people some of the time but you shouldn't be seeking to fool them at all.
>
> **Business Perspective:** Successful organizations understand that all their members are intuitive and creative individuals. They know and understand the organization through its leaders and managers. To assume anything less of them will impact on profitability. Customers are also intuitive and make choices about which organizations they will support. This demands that organizational leaders and managers follow an ethical and moral vision.

Lead with integrity

The most important ingredient in effective leadership is integrity. People will not follow you if they can see through you and your policies.

They will be inspired if they can see into who you are and why you do what you say. Leadership with integrity has to be done in a way that allows leaders to be true to themselves and the work that they have been called to undertake.

Show you are committed

All leadership requires vision and commitment. Jesus led with integrity into the most difficult of places. He spoke of people not looking or turning back once they had put their hand to the plough. All those who take up new work wonder at some time if they have done the right thing. The job is never completely as described.

The people you work with, God's gift in that place, are never quite as they appeared at first, but neither are the opportunities and the rewards. Pieces of work done with others in a committed and trusting atmosphere bring surprising and greater returns. This is the effective atmosphere in which committed people can feel God's Spirit at work.

Be true to yourself

Effective personal leadership brings a sense of well-being. A leader with vision can be caricatured and undermined by critics who do not share the vision. Reactions have to demonstrate inclusiveness and the will and ability to listen to comment and criticism. Integrity can be known and understood through a sense of well-being. God was well pleased when Jesus was commissioned for ministry at his baptism. The Bible uses the same word for God's pleasure and blessing at the scene of the transfiguration. Those whom God calls he also blesses with skills and abilities.

There are the varieties of gifts that Paul speaks of and which are present in every Christian community. Effective leaders use their own gifts to mobilize and liberate the gifts of others.

Know when to go

Leadership with integrity also demands the wisdom to know when to end a piece of work and when to leave a post or a church. Jesus warned that not everyone will always be welcomed in every community. Different skills are needed at different times and not all policies and personalities fit every situation. Occasionally the time comes to 'shake the dust off one's feet' and go to another place. Effectiveness and integrity can be shown in appropriate endings and in choosing not to avoid difficult decisions.

Listen and learn

The measure of effectiveness is in open and trusting consultation. Leaders who listen, consult and who explain their decisions have the potential to be effective and to make many people feel they are in the right place at the right time.

For reflection and discussion

1 What is a leader?
2 What kind of leader was Jesus?
3 How is the leadership style of Jesus represented in your church?
4 How is the leadership style of Jesus represented in your own life?

Great Idea 20

Be Witnesses in the Workplace

JOHN NELSON

> The harvest is plentiful but the workers are few
> Matthew 9.37
>
> **Top Tip:** Go to the customer, don't wait for the customer to come to you.
>
> **Business Perspective:** Successful organizations understand the value of indirect marketing. They train their staff to positively represent their organization at all times and in the most unlikely places. No opportunity is missed to promote the organization profitably.

One of the most common challenges facing Christians is how to reach out and promote their faith in their work situation. Too often churches are trapped in their own cultural heritage and expressions of faith are limited to their attendance at worship.

A new perspective flows from being free from the historical and structural ties of the organization. While the church infrastructure is important it should not be viewed as the primary instrument of mission.

Some churches have successfully recognized that the workplace is a mission field and offers ways of supporting its members for mission and ministry at work. However, ordained ministers need to recognize that they do have the capacity to maximize the potential for mission offered by places of work.

This requires that ordained ministers adopt a collaborative and supportive management style that equips church members to engage profitably in the workplace.

All too often church leaders say they believe the workplace is a mission field but fail to generate the capacity to engage successfully in this area. The workplace is often sidelined and yet for most people it is the place where they will spend most of their lives. The workplace represents the most important opportunity for mission.

Given that most people accept that the workplace is a mission field, relatively few churches have an implementable strategy. No one would dispute the need for training missionaries who travel abroad, and yet it seems that those working the biggest mission field are neither trained nor prepared for being missionaries right where they are.

Churches over the years have developed great ministries for helping the sick and disadvantaged of our society even though a relatively small number of congregations will ever participate in this work. Some churches have achieved great breakthroughs in social justice but most remain quiet in supporting that place where most of the church's missionaries are called to serve, the ever-secular business environment.

It is not enough for churches to remember to pray for their parishioners in the workplace. They must also be prepared to offer practical help and support to enable each to function as witnesses at work.

Every mission-minded church must have a strategic plan for enabling its members to be effective witnesses at work. Such a plan must be built around achievability, sustainability and acceptability and may include the following:

1   A teaching programme on discipleship and witness at work.
2   A prayer group for workplace witnesses.
3   The inclusion of prayers for people at work.
4   A special service and pastoral care for the workplace.
5   The marking of celebrations in the workplace.

The benefits are obvious: profitability. Profitable for the individual, profitable for the workplace and profitable for the church.

For reflection and discussion

1 How much direct involvement has your church had with places of work.
2 How much would you have to do to implement a witness at work strategy?
3 What measures can you use to assess the profitability of your workplace strategy?
4 What level of commitment are you able to give to witness at work strategy?

Great Idea 21

Bring God into Everyday Life

ELIZABETH MATEAR

Be outward looking, see the opportunities around. If we keep doing what we do we will keep getting what we get. Our sole purpose, to follow Jesus and mission, will be the result. Bring God into everyday life.

Great Idea 22

Care for the Co-habiting

REBECCA PAVELEY

Be kind and compassionate to one another, forgiving each other,
just as in Christ God forgave you
Ephesians 4.32

Top Tip: What is needed is a theology of marriage rather than
assume that marriage is the default position.

Business Perspective: Successful organizations understand
that markets are not static. They strive to create products that
meet the needs of their customers rather than sustain their
own organizational culture. Sometimes all this requires is a
repackaging of the product with customer-appropriate language.

For advocates of traditional marriage, statistics paint a bleak
picture of relationship trends in Britain today: the number of
marriages is steadily declining, while the number of couples choosing to cohabit increases exponentially. The Office for National
Statistics 2007 survey found the number of couples cohabiting
had risen by around 16 per cent over the last two decades and is
projected to continue to rise.

While the Church of England and its clergy struggle to adapt
to this new relationship climate, their congregation do not. Many
are cohabiting before marriage. Some older couples – either after
a divorce or widowhood – are choosing not to marry again when
they meet someone else.

Theologians who have researched the increase in cohabitation say there is evidence that couples who belong to a church do think more carefully before they move in together. Duncan Dormor, Dean of Chapel, St John's College, Cambridge observes that for a lot of people who enter into a cohabiting relationship that is committed, marriage is quite clearly on the agenda. This is particularly true of Christians who cohabit.

The figures also show that two-thirds of cohabiting relationships converted to marriage. So it is a bridge for people and it is widespread among Christians, apart perhaps from the sectarian end of the Church.

Marriage used to be a very different affair. Our notions of what is traditional, white weddings and no sex before the ceremony, date back only to Victorian times.

It was only in 1754, when the Marriage Act came into force, that a marriage ceremony was compulsory in England and Wales. Before this, betrothals were the beginning of a marriage, followed later by the nuptials. Sexual relations followed the betrothal and children born to the betrothed couple were legitimate.

Some theologians urge clergy to talk in the church about cohabitation. They argue that the church either is helpful to people or it makes them feel guilty, or it simply has nothing to say. Others criticize the church for pastoral neglect and even incompetence for its lack of clear direction to couples who cohabit. What is needed is a theology of marriage rather than assume that marriage is the default position.

Healthy churches need a healthy and biblical approach to relationships. The following points should be noted.

1 Marriage is no longer the default position of the sexually active.
2 The Church should be basing its sexual teaching around marriage.
3 The Church should be teaching the idea of marriage as a covenant. For example Rowan Williams talks about loving couples loving one another as God loves us.

In its defence, the Church has attempted to respond to shifting patterns of relationships by bringing out a new liturgy for Marriage with Baptism, which recognizes that for many couples, the birth of the child makes them think about marriage.

This has been attacked by some on the conservative wing, who see it as giving tacit approval to sex outside marriage.

For many people marriage is seen largely in terms of what it offers any children. So, governments are happy to say they support marriage as the statistics show it offers the most stability for children and therefore the best social and economic outlook.

For reflection and discussion

1 What in your view constitutes marriage?
2 What does the Bible teach about marriage?
3 How can your church best support those who choose not to marry in the traditional sense?
4 What 'business' is it anyway, of the Church, if people choose not to marry but demonstrate a committed loving and lifelong relationship?

Great Idea 23

Change the Way we Make Decisions

PATRICK GOH

> I will pour out my Spirit on all people. Your sons and daughters will prophesy, your old men will dream dreams, your young men will see visions
> Joel 2.28

Top Tip: Finding common ground has a strong and binding effect on the organization.

Business Perspective: Successful organizations understand that decision making is often impeded by individual personalities driven by strong personal agendas. Such decision-making processes often fulfil the individual's needs rather than those of the organization. Such organizations spend time and effort on training and encouraging managers to consider the needs of the organization and others before their own.

How do you lead if God has empowered everyone to prophesy, dream dreams and see visions?

Part of the answer is to make decision making a relational process. This can be done by designing activities that help people think and talk communally. The notion of involving everyone in decision making fits with emerging relational theories that emphasize communal sense making.

Relational thinking involves getting your whole system working on important issues. This is really hard work but probably the only way to make use of the wisdom of groups and to create shared ownership. It is based on the notion that finding common ground has a binding and generative effect on people. The process enables diverse groups to arrive at agreements about the future they want, and the actions to achieve it.

However, existing power relationships tend to get in the way of relational practice. There are a number of ways to interfere with this pattern.

A fun but effective method for developing relational thinking in your meetings is to issue people with an equal amount of Lego. Each time someone speaks, the individual would forfeit a brick. Once a participant has used their allocated bricks, they simply have to listen to the contribution of the others. Be prepared for significant reactions to this powerful management tool. You may like to use this as a training exercise before implementing it into your management meetings. Take good note of the following incident that occurred in a church management meeting.

In the middle of a contribution by a woman participant, a bishop who had used up his bricks declared that he was not going to follow the rules as he still had a lot more to say.

This sparked a fierce debate about the point of the bricks. Amid the heated discussion the woman who was in mid-sentence when the bishop interrupted broke down in tears. Sobbing uncontrollably, she said that this was typical of her experience; ignored, undervalued, with people speaking over her as though she wasn't there.

Tension filled the room. Another participant then went up to the woman hugged her and said that he sympathized, as this was how he felt as well.

The bishop who disrupted the conversation apologized. This emboldened others who did not normally speak in public. The unease turned into a feeling that new ground was being charted. The conversation that followed seemed to be filled with possibilities and the mood created. People expressed the feeling that the very nature of the organization was being changed by what was happening.

For reflection and discussion

1 At your last meeting what most influenced the decision-
   making process, the relationships or the individual
   agendas?
2 How much time do you spend on building relationships in
   your church?
3 How might you best use the Lego brick tool?
4 How do you measure the quality of the relationships
   within your church management meetings?

Great Idea 24

Come for Tea, Come for Tea, my People!

IVOR TELFER

> Behold I stand at the door and knock
> Revelation 3.20
>
> **Top Tip:** Always focus on the person not the project.
>
> **Business Perspective:** Successful business organizations understand that attracting customers requires marketing strategies that speak to them in their language and importantly create an environment in which they feel comfortable operating. Attracting customers and keeping them is a major business challenge.

Apart from the fact that medical experts have recently commented that cups of tea don't do people any harm, a Christian cup of tea can be a really special tool.

Most people will be aware of the great work done by The Salvation Army during the two world wars with their cups of tea, often at or near the front line. What is needed is a front-line attitude in today's world where something as simple as a cup of tea can make a difference.

Many of the problems in our society can be met in some measure by simple human contact, for example over a cup of tea, a Christian cup of tea.

Here's what to do.

Have a cup of tea with someone you don't know very well and

who perhaps already exists on the fringe of the local community. This is an easy way to start building a relationship with this person and meeting them at their point of need.

Without doubt this is a scary prospect so personal safety is essential. Make sure that you do not make yourself too vulnerable so when choosing the person you should:

1 Pray for God to point out someone to you whom you already know at least a little.
2 Invite or offer to visit for a cup of tea (and let someone else know you are doing this). This not only helps your security but may also encourage them to either share a cup of tea with someone or to come along too.
3 Be yourself and be really natural. Don't be offended by a refusal.
4 Think about some things to chat about that you may have in common, for example your school-age children or grandchildren, your work, etc. Don't worry if God or the church doesn't come into the conversation – there is plenty of time.
5 Without interrogating the person, find out a bit more about them by telling them about yourself first. (Don't share your testimony with them yet – wait until they ask.)
6 Over time build a relationship with that person on a regular basis and keep praying for them and the information you have learned about them.
7 Remember that the aim of this is to make a difference in another person's life. It is not a recruitment drive.

Your priority is the person but it may be that one day they may want to come to church or come back to church. Pray that at some time they will want to do just that and prepare for it. Here are some tips:

1 Let your minister know and agree the best time to come. Not all church services are appropriate for first timers or returners. Don't invite someone on the stewardship day or day of the Annual Parochial Church Meeting.

2 Offer to provide transport if needed, or go with them and sit with them as much as possible and also make sure you have called a few friends so they know you are bringing someone with you and can make sure they chat to them.

3 When people come to church for the first time, they need five good conversations with different people each week for the first three weeks to make sure they feel welcome. That's 15 conversations with different people, not just 'Hello, how are you?' but real conversations – not too long though!

It often takes about four years for someone to come to faith in Christ so don't be discouraged if things aren't happening as quickly as you had hoped. It could happen over your first Christian cup of tea or it may take a lot longer. The most important thing is your friendship, the rest is up to God.

For reflection and discussion

1 Who in your church or community do you know who would value friendly contact and support?
2 How good is your church at welcoming visitors?
3 Why should your church engage in such activity?
4 What encourages you or discourages you from inviting non-Christians to your church?

Great Idea 25

Count the Cost

KEITH WILLIAMS

> Will they not first sit down and estimate the cost
> to see if they have enough money to complete the task?
> Luke 14.28

Top Tip: Finance vision and strategy are inseparable.

Business Perspective: Successful organizations understand that monetary profit is vital to their continued existence; however they recognize that it is not the sole measure of profit. Included in this metric will be things such as public opinion, conformance, good governance and stakeholder approval.

There are many similarities between how you manage the finances of a church and any other organization. There is a need to exercise stewardship by planning income, expenditure and cash flow. There is also a need to control transactions on a day-to-day basis and keep proper records, so the skills of a book-keeper/accountant are valuable to the treasurer. The big difference for a church however is a mindset which requires a very different approach and looking in the right direction.

The objective of a church is not to solely to make a monetary profit, break even or preserve the status quo, but it is to grow God's kingdom.

It is not ultimately accountable to any person, or group of people, but to Christ, and the real cost has already been paid by Christ on the cross. We are stewards of what God has given to us because everything comes from him. Therefore our mindset must be about discerning what God wants us to do; being obedient to his will by spending what he wants us to spend; and trusting him to provide all the resources that we need – even though some will see this as foolishness.

You can't drive a car by looking in the rear-view mirror – that only shows you where you have been but doesn't show you where you are going. Similarly we must beware of managing the finances of our churches by looking at the past. What we spent last year may be interesting and may help us to understand some of our costs, but it should not be used to determine what we spend in the future to grow a healthy church.

We need to be open to new ideas and initiatives that will move us forward and not be constrained by preserving the status quo.

The plans to deliver the vision and strategy, with estimates of all the costs involved, should be our starting point for developing our expenditure budgets and cash-flow forecasts. We should then add the ongoing costs of existing activities and infrastructure that are essential for the work of the church. The budget should be subjected to challenge and prayer by the leadership team and the whole congregation to determine if it represents God's plan and priorities.

We need to move forward in faith and look out for confirmation that we are on the right track, and for income, sometimes from unexpected sources. We need to communicate clearly and widely what God has called us to do; how much it will cost, and what income we need to meet the costs. Throughout the year we need to communicate progress made against plans, and the income received, and to be open to indications that God wants us to change direction.

For reflection and discussion

1 Why is it important to financially balance the books?
2 What are your current revenue streams?
3 How will you generate income in the future?
4 Where are the skills in your church for managing money?

Great Idea 26

Create a Community Arts Project

A Case Study

PAUL DAVIES

Over the last 12 months at St Mary's Church we have made a concerted push to put the church at the centre of our community to get the people of Sunbury to engage with the church in a dynamic and spiritual way. We achieved this goal by orchestrating two art-based projects; ideas that could connect and unify local groups and cultivate a positive association with the church.

Our first project, Sunbury Swans, involved five local primary schools. During just one week in July, each school with the assistance of a local artist, designed and built their own large wicker swan, approximately 6ft long and 5ft high. With the River Thames running through Sunbury, the swan is very much a symbol of our community.

Upon their completion, the church space was cleared whereupon the five swans were placed upon a vast blue material surface to represent the river. During that Saturday morning and afternoon, the swans received visitors in their hundreds; this included the children and teachers involved, along with the children's families and members of the local community in general. A number of people commented that they had experienced a calming atmosphere of spirituality. In the early evening, local air cadets gave the swans a procession down to the river where the models were tied to small boats and subsequently towed along the river accompanied by music from Swan Lake. For the next few weeks the swans were on display at a public garden at the heart of Sunbury village; a well-received exhibition that included a workshop on how the swans were created.

Our second project was called Jigsaw of Community Life and followed a similar method to our first event. The concept, a collaborative artwork in the form of large-scale interlocking jigsaw pieces, again incorporated five Sunbury primary schools. Each one received a pre-cut jigsaw-shaped piece of MDF and were then asked to produce a colourful design which celebrated the positive aspects and themes of school, family and Sunbury community life.

Upon completion, all five pieces, rich with vibrant drawings and collages, were unified and displayed together at St Mary's Church for community viewing. They were later exhibited at the public gardens. Most beautifully and poignantly, it was sometimes hard to see where one piece started and another began.

Both projects outlined here had an overwhelmingly positive effect on the community. The projects had enabled local children to have their creative skills appreciated, and expressed something of the life of our village through beautiful artistry. Indeed it was a particularly uplifting experience for the church itself. With St Mary's proving the catalyst behind these events and actively inviting many local groups to become involved, the church had positioned itself at the centre of the community and it had defined itself to Sunbury as a thriving source of creativity, partnership and harmony. We had connected positively with hundreds of local people, many of whom had never visited our church before on a scale and intimacy that perhaps would not have been possible with a church service. We had offered something quite different and in turn ignited a wonderful community feeling that gave ourselves, our participants and our visitors to Sunbury a spiritual sense of peace and well-being.

For reflection and discussion

1 What was the business case for St Mary's art project?
2 What do you think will be the future business benefits for St Mary's?

Great Idea 27

Create a Holiday Club

A Case Study

MICHAEL JAGESSAR AND
SANDRA ACKROYD

Once upon a time in 2009, sitting in a front room in South Ilford, the junior church leaders of Vine United Reformed Church were asking, 'How can we as a church engage with more children? We only have five or six in the church.'

One of the members had an idea. 'Have you thought of having something like a holiday club for a week during the August holidays?' The response was that the church had done so 25 years ago, but the area was different then and now they would not have enough leaders. However, six young adults in the church were willing to give it a go and saw it as a challenge.

A training day was held for the young leaders along with preparation sessions, to ensure that the team put in place good practice, including child protection concerns. The initiative was then advertised among the church user groups and in a few neighbourhood primary schools. The area had become very multicultural and multi-faith in recent years; and there were concerns as to what would result from our advertising.

Was it possible for a church to start such an initiative in a community that is multi-faith? Well, the registration forms rolled in abundantly. The children of the church responded, as did a few children with no faith background or church connection. However, the majority of the children came from Muslim, Hindu and

Sikh families. The publicity explicitly stated that the theme and ethos had a Christian faith basis, while noting that all the different faith backgrounds of the children would be respected. It also noted that this was an opportunity to learn from one another in sport, drama, craft, dance, cooking and outings, etc. The holiday club was a complete success.

August came and before the end of the holiday club a parent asked whether the children would have to wait a whole year before meeting each other again. Parents and children had already decided there would be another holiday club in 2010, but wished for something in-between. Was there a much bigger challenge here than the group had realized? We had the inspiration and motivation to start a Saturday club for children once a month. Since the 2009 holiday club and throughout the monthly Saturday gatherings a strong relationship has been built up with the children and many of their parents.

Parents have been quite vocal in saying what they feel about this initiative. One parent said, 'This is the only opportunity my child gets outside school of mixing in an informal way with children of different cultures and faiths and I think this is important.' Another took time to affirm the leaders, 'You are doing a really good bit of social cohesion here.' The small group did not realize that was what they were doing.

In the programmes, stories and discussion arise and spirituality is regularly explored. On one Saturday a nine-year-old Hindu girl said, 'The important thing in life is to have a free spirit, freed from negative thinking.'

Other outcomes include the development of leadership and skills of the young adults who managed the holiday club. Another outcome is the building of self-esteem and confidence and the building of relationships and trust with and among parents.

Undergirding this whole enterprise has been the prayer and support of the church. The leaders took a risk, faced challenges, overcame fears and difficulties while noting that there may be more on the way; but the view is that all have been surprised by joy and are still learning as they dare to move forward on this exciting adventure.

For reflection and discussion

1 What was the business case for Vine URC creating a holiday club?
2 What do you think will be the future business benefits for Vine URC as a consequence of this iniative?

Great Idea 28

Delegate with Confidence

RICHARD DANNATT

Ideally, ordained ministers should aim to concentrate their efforts on the spiritual needs of their congregation. They can do this better if they have the confidence to delegate routine administrative tasks to competent lay members. Clergy and laity can then work as a genuine team.

Great Idea 30

Develop and Grow Together

ROGER BUSH

Rural churches and communities can often feel isolated and remote, but by working together, as we are beginning to do in Cornwall, two things happen: you discover that you can gain expertise from a neighbouring parish that you don't have yourselves, so it is perfectly possible for one person to do several parishes' accounts, or be a buildings' officer for several churches; and you find your vision opening up, seeing God's grace at work in other communities. You realize that you are not on your own and that he is at work everywhere. In an age when the rural economy is under threat, that vision is never more important.

Great Idea 31

Develop the Talents of Others

ROY BAKER

The essence of leadership and management in a church is to discover and develop talents in others which you haven't got yourself. In doing so, don't get in the way of the Holy Spirit by trying to do God's work for him. Remember what happened to Paul when he tried to go into Bithynia! (Acts 16.7).

Great Idea 32

Distil Some Passion Stew!

JOHN KINGSLEY MARTIN

> All things come from you and of your own do we give you
> 1 Chronicles 29.14
>
> **Top Tip:** No one individual has a monopoly, either on good ideas or on interpretation of where the Holy Spirit is leading.
>
> **Business Perspective:** Successful organizations understand that the utilization of all available resources are vital to their profitability. However it is the productive combination of these resources that is the key management challenge.

During the Great Depression of the 1930s, American families hit hard by events they could not control lived on a dish called passion stew. It was made up of just about any ingredient that could be found on the day. They would simply collect it, throw it into a pot, and stir. The concoction apparently acquired the name passion stew because people said they would throw all their anxieties, worries and passions into the pot with the other ingredients.

We know that churches are packed full of people with strong ideas, convictions, passions.

- How can these be worked on so there is shared vision?
- How can we be sure that the best ideas are harvested?
- Are there ways to make sure that vision days are not simply plans imposed by the more powerful or articulate?

When it comes to sitting down together to fashion all this energy into some sort of shared vision we often simply end up in a stew. This recipe for distilling passion stew aims to share some practical advice on how to overcome some of these issues.

It is important to recognize that no one individual has a monopoly, either on good ideas or on interpretation of where the Holy Spirit is leading.

Without doubt the apostle Paul found the church in Corinth the most difficult of all. There were factions. There was flagrant immorality. There were those who claimed to be 'super apostles' with knowledge superior even to Paul himself. And yet the apostle recognizes that this community, in itself, possessed all the requisite spiritual gifts for its flourishing. All of Paul's dealings with the Corinthians is predicated on this assumption.

Church leaders today need to recognize that this principle is true in the life of every church community. They need to strive to recognize, accept and manage the ingredients that will already exist in their church.

For reflection and discussion

1 What gifts and talents are available to you for the successful management of your church?
2 How do you ensure that everyone in your church has a voice and is heard?
3 What does the recipe for your church's passion stew contain?
4 In what quantities are your ingredients?

Great Idea 33

Do it for Them not for Yourself

MICHAEL LOFTHOUSE AND
ANTON MÜLLER

As I walked around and surveyed your objects of worship I found an altar with an inscription to an unknown god. What you worship as something unknown I am going to proclaim to you
Acts 17.23

Top Tip: Place your church in the market.

Business Perspective: Successful commercial businesses design products for their customers not for themselves. It is surprising that most church organizations fail to see the potential market that is on their own doorstep. This kind of neglect is the inevitable outcome of the kind of introspective management that is endemic in churches across the UK.

If churches knew who their customers were and what products they required to facilitate their spiritual health and well-being would they really continue to offer the current goods and services? By designing and delivering products that target the needs of the customer profitably, in other words, church growth would be achieved and the mission of the church would be further advanced.

Any business, before embarking upon its enterprise, would first of all survey the potential market to understand what goods and services it needs to offer in order to generate a profitable outcome.

Within a short walk of the average town church in the UK there will be 10,000-plus people which will include the following customer segments:

- 1,200 people living alone, of whom 580 will be of pensionable age
- 1,500 people who talk to their neighbours less than once a week
- 50 people who have been divorced within the last year
- 375 single parents
- 18 pregnant teenagers
- 150 recent or contemplated abortions
- 250 people who are unemployed
- 1,700 people living in low income households
- 1,100 people with some kind of mental disorder
- 100 bereavements within the last year
- 2,700 people living in households without a car
- 60 people in a residential care home
- 1,280 people caring for a sick, disabled or elderly relative or friend
- 2,800 people who have been victims of crime in the past year
- 40 homeless people
- 15 asylum seekers.

This kind of market research is the starting point for any church wishing to meet the social and spiritual needs of the community it is trying to reach. This will prompt a radical reassessment of the current service provision of the church. This kind of market research and product development is a relatively simple process.

However, there is an overriding management imperative.

Before engaging in this process your church must be structurally, culturally and spiritually prepared. Only then can the existing church community accept the changes that are necessary to accommodate the certain growth that will follow this kind of radical intervention and interaction with the community.

In management terms it is easy to attract customers: keeping them is hard. In the church context this process needs to facilitate growth while taking care of the existing church community.

For reflection and discussion

1 How would you design a service that is feasible and sustainable for any three of the above customer segments?
2 How will you prepare your church for this kind of intervention?
3 What criteria of assessment will you use to measure your desired outcome?
4 What leadership and management will you require?

Great Idea 34

Do the Things that Matter

PETER BATES

Commit to the Lord all that you do and your plans will be fulfilled
Proverbs 16.3

Top Tip: Know what to do and what not to do.

Business Perspective: Successful organizations understand the destructive force of costs on profitability and strive to do only that which is profitable. Time spent on non-profitable activities not only wastes money but drains the creative potential of the organization.

Most of us, especially those in church circles or voluntary activities, occasionally get overwhelmed by a multitude of tasks, and we need to practise some 'planned neglect'. If you want something done ask a busy person goes the old adage. From time to time we need to sit back and take stock, setting some priorities for the many tasks that we have in hand.

Here are three standard management questions that you will find helpful:

1 What am I doing that does not need to be done at all?
2 Which of my activities could be handled just as well or better by someone else?
3 What do I do that wastes other people's time?

It is worth asking these questions at regular and set intervals during the year, going through all your current and pending activities in a disciplined and methodical way. Look through those papers in your in-tray; check again that 'to do' list. There will inevitably be some items that belong to question one and can be dropped immediately.

Question two demands that the leader engages fully in the delegation of tasks. It is here where many leaders, and most often church leaders, struggle. Effective delegation takes time and must be handled thoughtfully and strategically. It raises the possibility that others may be better at some things than yourself. A good manager will welcome and celebrate this. A good manager is someone who is able to identify the best people for the task which needs doing. A poor manager is one who believes that the only way to get something done properly is to do it yourself. Churches are full of DIY leaders and it shows.

Question three deals with the impact of the management of our work on others. Being unprepared for meetings is a common example of where leaders waste the time of others. Another example is the all too often practice of delegating those tasks which should have been dropped. Other people are often much better at spotting the wasteful and irrelevant things that we do. It is insulting and demoralizing to simply pass those things on to the very people who know that the task is unimportant and need not be done.

For reflection and discussion

1 What methods do you use for prioritizing your work and others' work?
2 What is most likely to distract you from your priorities?
3 What methods do you employ to overcome distractions?
4 How would you rate your effectiveness in completing your priorities?

Great Idea 35

Don't be Suspicious of Economics

BERNARD FOLEY

You have been faithful with a few things;
I will put you in charge of many things
Matthew 25.21

Top Tip: Trust is a fundamental feature of economic life.

Business Perspective: Successful organizations understand that they are not immune from the influences of the social, economic and political environment in which they operate. Monitoring and understanding this constantly changing environment allows organizations to understand and work within the constraints which the environment generates. It also reveals the opportunities for creative thinking and increased profitability.

Church leaders and indeed many Christians look at the subject of economics with some degree of suspicion or even hostility. Why?

Much of its subject seems to deal with human beings as if they were entirely egocentric, materialistic calculating machines. Competition and the neo-Darwinist 'survival of the fittest' seem to be the order of the day. Often economic policies are proposed which run counter to Judeo-Christian ethics on caring for the poor and the importance of other directed behaviour.

The impersonal 'invisible' hand of the market has been seen as the centrepiece of economic ideas. Some of the worst aspects of this kind of thinking came to the surface in the last couple of decades with the emphasis on privatization and deregulation.

This was followed in the field of banking leading to the financial crisis that erupted in 2008, the consequences of which will continue to reverberate for years.

While this mode of thinking has been undoubtedly a feature of traditional economics, it is by no means the complete picture. For many years there have been dissenting voices. For example the idea of the 'economic external' which is central to modern welfare economics and environmentalism.

A popular phrase to characterize this view was 'Spaceship Earth' to signify the problem of finite resources and wider ecological concerns. This view has also been called 'Small is Beautiful' which inspired a series of new ideas on tackling problems on the human scale.

But perhaps the most significant development, however, was the emergence of Game Theory. This focused on decision making among small groups of people and organizations. The crucial feature of the game situation is that decisions are interdependent. Game Theory is the study of interactive decision making; that is, in situations where each person's action affects the outcome for the whole group.

In the early stages, most of the games analysed were the one-off zero sum non-co-operative games where rational self-interest remained the dominant paradigm.

Even in the simplest cases, the so-called prisoner's dilemma, it was soon shown that if the game is played repeatedly, co-operation between the parties becomes the outcome.

Hence, the benefits of co-operation outweigh those of individualistic self-seeking behaviour. Trust is a fundamental feature of economic life just as much as is rivalry and competition.

Game theory can be employed to show the advantages of trust, reciprocity and mutuality. It has proved useful in informing a wide range of economic and political issues. It is also applicable across a whole series of social and political problems, such as how to approach peace negotiations.

It would appear that society has moved from the more selfish interest of the economic man to the more inclusive and collaborative style of 'behavioural economics'.

It is therefore vitally important that church leaders and managers recognize this paradigm shift and harness the opportunities that this new society offers.

For reflection and discussion

1 How aware are you of the concept of behavioural economics and its relevance to your church?
2 What strategies have you in place to harness a more collaborative society to improve the profitability of your church?
3 Who in your church is best placed to assist you in this process?
4 What evidence is there of this paradigm shift in your community?

Great Idea 36

Don't Recruit – Evangelize!

ANTON MÜLLER

Ask the Lord of the harvest to send out workers into his harvest field
Matthew 9.38

Top Tip: Evangelism serves the mission of God whereas recruitment serves the mission of church.

Business Perspective: Successful commercial business organizations recognize that their culture is pervasive and can be corrosive. They work hard to ensure that their culture drives their mission, values their workforce and creates a positive and profitable working environment.

It is not uncommon for church cultures to demand conformity from its workforce. While adherence to productive rules is important such cultures can have a negative effect and are epitomized by such remarks as, 'We see your role as attracting new people and assimilating them into the way we do things round here.'

Such a culture will stifle entrepreneurship and creativity, it will make people unhappy resulting in an unprofitable workforce and ultimately an unhealthy church. An unhealthy church can be epitomized by such remarks as, 'It's the social calibre of the people who you are attracting that concerns us.'

When a part of the church community attempts to move the organization forward profitably they are met with an impenetrable wall of cultural resistance. There is often a dichotomy of what is said and what is done.

Such thinking will not exist in isolation and the attentive manager can quickly establish the nature of the organizational culture by listening to this informal communication. Here lies the real culture of the organization which is often not revealed through the formal structures and dialogues such as the parish profile.

The culture is one of serving itself rather than meeting the needs of the community and is often evident structurally through falling numbers in the congregation. So what has happened to the command of Jesus to the fledgling church to go out to baptize and to teach.

Somewhere along the way the church has replaced the command to evangelize with the desire to recruit. Is it so different? Surely it is just another way of saying the same thing; to bring people into the church?

The difference is very subtle which makes it all the more insidious. Consider these subtle differences: evangelism serves others but recruitment serves itself; recruitment asks people to come into church while evangelism asks the church to go out to people; evangelism serves the mission of God whereas recruitment serves the mission of the church.

There may be nothing wrong with that, where the mission of the church is in line with the mission of God. It's a subtle difference but one which has led many churches away from fulfilling God's purpose for the church in the community and the world.

However, the problems are clear and therefore manageable when you compare the fundamental elements of each style of church:

The Evangelizing Church	The Recruiting Church
Will focus on ministry to others	Will focus on ministry to itself
Will focus on planting and nurturing community-based groups	Will focus on keeping the show on the road
Will focus on giving	Will focus on income
Will focus on discipleship and equipping	Will focus on numbers

Will focus on Word and Sacrament	Will focus on religious practice and ritual
Will focus on developing lay participation and leadership	Will focus on the ministry of the few or the one

It may be tempting to link the recruiting church and the evangelistic church with a particular kind of tradition but that would be wrong. An evangelical church by tradition may not necessarily be an evangelistic church. A church with a pattern of traditions and rituals may be very active in the service of the community.

It's not about high church, low church, the Book of Common Prayer, Common Worship, traditional hymns, new songs. It's about whether a church is in recruiting mode or evangelistic mode. A recruiting church will be set in its own ways whereas an evangelistic church will be set on God's ways.

If the reason for increasing Sunday attendance is about paying the quota, maintaining the building or keeping a worthy tradition going in your locality then your church is most likely stuck in recruitment mode.

Social institutions recruit and are often bound by a club mentality that requires its members to conform to a way of being that preserves the club, its traditions and values.

To be healthy, churches must operate from an evangelistic outlook as the basis for growth.

For reflection and discussion

1 What does an evangelizing church look like for you?
2 What do you need to do to create an evangelizing church?
3 What do you need to do to be the leader of an evangelizing church?
4 What criteria will you use to assess the success of an evangelizing church?

Great Idea 37

Don't Throw out the Baby with the Baptism Water

ALAN BILLINGS

> As they travelled along the road together they
> came to some water
> Acts 8.36
>
> **Top Tip:** The customer comes first.
>
> **Business Perspective:** Successful organizations understand that there is no substitute for a quality product if long-term profitability is to be achieved. Quality is judged by the customer not the organization and first impressions always count. Essential to a quality product is constant monitoring through customer surveys as a way of keeping up with and satisfying customer needs. A contented customer will not only recommend an organization to others but may also buy other products that the organization offers.

No one disputes that we live in a more secular culture, though not one that is dead to the things of the Spirit. It is not a totally materialistic culture, though people no longer naturally look to the churches for spiritual resource. It follows, therefore, that those occasions where the ministry of the church is sought, weddings, baptisms, funerals, are highly significant.

Christianity has something of value that cannot be found elsewhere. How can we make the pastoral offices better occasions for genuinely pastoral ministry? We need to discover as far as we can why people come. Dealing well with people at these times is one way in which perceptions of the church can be shaped at grass-roots level.

Parents who bring their children for baptism are not coming to join the church. They are coming to express through word and symbolic action what they think and feel about the birth of their child and what they hope for their future.

The function of Christian ministry at this point is to help them do that. We cannot second guess what is in their mind. So here is a suggestion for managing baptisms as ministry and mission.

1 Create a small team of lay volunteers who will make the pastoral care of infant baptism families their ministry.
2 Each volunteer visits a family to complete the application form and talk with them about their child.
3 During the course of this conversation ask a few key questions as part of the natural flow of talking.
   • What does this child mean for you?
   • What do you hope for them?
   • What is there about a service in church that is important for you?
   They may struggle to articulate this.

Those involved will be astonished by what they find that will give spiritual meaning and value to the ministry being requested. For example: the unmarried mother who needs to prove to herself that she can be a good parent; the child that is the result of IVF after many years; the couple who had been struggling within the marriage see this as a second chance; the family in which a much loved grandfather has just died.

Team and clergy meet before the baptism to share what has been learned and to decide on an appropriate reading, prayers and music. Finding appropriate Scripture readings and composing suitable prayers is a good, if testing, exercise for the team! At the service the team member greets the family, reads the lesson, says the prayers and presents the baptism candle.

From time to time, the team reviews what has been learned and discuss 'why do people bring children for baptism?' The reasons may be different every time.

For reflection and discussion

1 What may be the obstacles in establishing a clergy and team approach to pastoral ministries?
2 How might these obstacles be overcome?
3 What changes may you have to make to your present management and leadership structure in your church to accommodate the development of pastoral lay teams?
4 How might your church benefit from adopting such an approach to the pastoral ministries?

Great Idea 38

Dream Dreams

PHIL SIMPSON

> I will pour out my Spirit on all people. Your sons and daughters
> will prophesy, your young men will see visions, your old men
> will dream dreams
> Acts 2.17

Top Tip: Collaborative processes generate corporately owned
knowledge.

Business Perspective: Successful organizations understand that
their competitive edge rests upon collaborative organizational-
wide knowledge generation and management.

Individuals dream, but what about congregations? How do you
capture the corporate dream of a group of God's people? The
whole not just a part?

One methodology is called Appreciative Enquiry. This may
be used in many contexts to enable groups to explore their joint
vision of what they want to achieve together.

Appreciative Enquiry works in four stages:

1 What is: Ask members and potential members of the church
to describe or discover the best of what is by telling individual stories of what has worked within their context and then
drawing out principles. This is based on the belief that organizations turn to what gives them life. It is not problem focused.
2 What could be: Ask members of the church to dream about

what can be. Think about what these ideas and principles will look like in the future.

3 Design 'what could be' by creating a doable road map for the future.
4 Deliver 'what will be' through a series of small actions that bring about the desired change.

This can work for groups of 10 to 20 people or even congregations of 150 to 200. Larger groups just take more time. The key is handling the process and enabling all present to have a say in what is being produced.

A methodology for implementing the four stages is the newspaper exercise. Having shared stories of what works in pairs, get pairs to join together in the group. The group review the principles and are given a task of producing a newspaper dated three, five, seven years into the future, depending on the vision process. The newspaper should be given a name, headlines, small articles and even pictures.

The format of the newspaper is not set and could include international news, local news, sport, cartoon, obituary, award ceremony. Anything. The overriding aim of the exercise is to allow the group to be creative while connecting to the stories of what has already worked.

The groups are then invited to share their newspapers with the rest of the people present. This process can generate a lot of hilarity and laughter, which in turn produces a sense of energy and connectedness leading to strong relational thinking and cohesive teams.

The newspapers then form the basis of group discussion to explore if that is where they want to head and what the group want to see in the future and how to get there.

This is an invaluable process for informing strategic and operational thinking. It is an effective tool for generating concrete and focused outcomes.

The final stage is to agree what the organization will do next.

This collaborative process generates corporately owned knowledge and provides rich material for leadership teams to craft the organization's vision statements and strategic plans. The voices of the organization have been heard and the individuals can recognize their input.

For reflection and discussion

1 What collaborative processes do you employ in your church to craft your church's vision and strategies?
2 How does your methodology compare with the newspaper method?
3 How will you prepare your church members to engage in such a process?
4 How will prepare yourself to manage such an envisioning process?

Great Idea 39

Dreams in Metaphors and Stories for Organizational Change

A Case Study

MARGARET HALSEY

When I had been in my current post for about three months as director of the Leeds Church Institute, I had a very vivid dream. I was returning from a holiday on a Greek island. I could not get everything into my suitcase and the flight was leaving in less than two hours. I woke from it with a start. I was convinced it had something to do with work but was rather unclear how or why this was the case.

When I went into work that morning I asked the staff, volunteer and paid alike, what my dream might mean. They all told me how they thought it mirrored our work. They offered many ideas and insights that were directly related to work load and prioritization.

I wondered if this process of interpretation of dream and associated metaphor could be applied elsewhere and so I tried it out with the council of the Leeds Church Institute.

I began by asking if they had a vision for where the organization might be going. I then shared my dream and invited them to suggest how they felt the dream might apply to the organization. I had noticed that a couple of the volunteers had said they found it hard to get into the work of the paid staff, and because I was also on a steep learning curve I shared that sense of not always being on top of detail.

So interpreting an unfinished dream was a way of levelling the ground and sharing ideas in a neutral arena in both contexts. All sorts of insights emerged about setting priorities: what should be in the suitcase; where the plane had come from and where it might be destined.

From this exercise I have retained two responses which in the end found expression in the work of the institute: Jesus said travel light, and the suggestion that we might 'drop the suitcase'. (Come unto me all who are weary and I shall give them rest.) Those two pieces of advice were enormously freeing.

The Leeds Church Institute was founded in 1857 as an educational charity by the Vicar of Leeds, Dr Walter Hook. It was initially founded as a resource for educating young people, a library and gathering place for its members and a focus of debate at the interface between the churches and contemporary society. But inevitably, although its core purposes remained constant, the forms and styles of activity had varied in different historical contexts. Its governance had become ecumenical and it had become involved in a wide variety of activities across the city. I was told that the main reason I had been appointed to the post was to help focus priorities and enable it to become more educationally focused in a different context.

I guess when I stop wondering about that it will be high time to pick up my suitcase up and travel on.

For reflection and discussion

1 What management implications emerge from the application of this metaphor?
2 What do you think will be the future management benefits for the Leeds Church Institute?

Great Idea 40

Embrace those on the Final Journey

SUE MÜLLER

As they talked and discussed these things with each other, Jesus
himself came up and walked along with them
Luke 24.15

Top Tip: A spiritually healthy church demonstrates unconditional
loving.

Business Perspective: Successful business organizations
understand that to be profitable they have to generate a loyal
customer base through committed and effective staff. Being seen
to undertake ethical and morally acceptable customer activities
generates such loyalty. But importantly such activities engender
a sense of well-being among the organization's staff which raise
productivity through the whole of the organization.

The Canadian Virtual Hospice website states:

A life-threatening illness can raise questions of meaning and
purpose in fresh and urgent ways and cause spiritual distress. If
you need palliative care, spiritual care may be as important to
your sense of well-being as physical care. Research has shown
that people with life threatening illnesses:

- consider their quality of life improved when their spiritual
  needs are addressed

- value and frequently use spiritual beliefs and practices as a way to help cope with their situation
- often want to talk about spiritual issues.

Many people explore spiritual questions near the end of life, searching for meaning and strength in relationships, and not only patients but also family members and friends may look for new ways to understand the fragility of life or express the depth of their caring when it seems to matter most. There are four questions which are most commonly stated:

1 Who will remember me?
2 What will they remember me for?
3 What memories can I still create?
4 Who am I really?

Churches need to be aware of the lonely and the vulnerable, the terminally ill and the long-term sick and housebound. Support is needed for those people who may appear to be coping with the situation as well as those who are not. Surely this is the bread and butter of church mission and ministry? It is an indicator of a well-managed and a well-led church, in tune with the spiritual needs of the community.

In some 30 years of nursing as a practice nurse, district nurse, hospice at home and hospice nurse it is evident that the church has been largely absent from the lives of the most lonely, the most vulnerable, the most frightened and the most spiritually isolated members of the community.

To add to the spiritual and pastoral neglect many funerals of patients attended over this time have been soul-less. The person, often unknown to the church leader, has been largely anonymous, hugely undervalued and denied dignity, respect and a lasting legacy for the community who remain.

When people attend a funeral they expect and are privileged to hear the most private and personal aspects of the life of the person who will have had an impact on their own lives. When a church leader fails to respect the integrity of the person and to replace their story with their own agenda they have not only failed that person they have failed to demonstrate their willingness to walk with the person who has a history and a story of their own. They have not modelled the ministry of Jesus.

The hallmark of Jesus' ministry was precisely this. When Jesus encountered suffering, pain and loss he was moved to compassion and did something about it. Jesus regularly encountered the spiritual needs of the community because he walked about among it. He walked with people and engaged with their stories.

Spiritual pain is almost always associated with different kinds of biographical distress which lead to a crisis of identity. The loss of one's personal story always reaches beyond that person to the family, friends and wider community.

A spiritually healthy, well-managed and well-led church is ideally placed to make available its resources of people and buildings to facilitate a space where people, irrespective of faith and belief, can find encouragement, support and love. A spiritually healthy church will be mindful of the importance of meeting the spiritual needs of the individual and the wider community.

The recommendation of this contribution to growing healthy churches is an appeal to churches to work directly with community care agencies to facilitate a safe place where people can meet. Here is the great idea: facilitate a HOPE group. This is a model initiated by the spiritual care co-ordinator of the Eden Valley Hospice some years ago and stands for Helping Others through Positive Encouragement.

Larry Culliford writing in *The Psychology of Spirituality* (Jessica Kingsley 2011) suggests that if we engage with the experience of others in the process of dying, death may become a vital and valuable teacher which prepares us to face its challenge. It may even appear to us at last as welcome as a friend.

It is a great opportunity for any church and is happening now, with you or without you.

For reflection and discussion

1 Is your church in a position to identify those in your community who are walking the last and quite often most loneliest of journeys?
2 How will you gain entry into the lives of people who are not part of your church group?
3 How will you make a connection and sustain that connection?
4 How will you ensure that your church is fit for purpose, that is, physically, emotionally, socially and spiritually equipped to walk as a companion with someone on their final journey?

Great Idea 41

Embrace Change

TIM HARLE

> The one who was seated on the throne said,
> 'See, I am making all things new'
> Revelation 21.5

Top Tip: Work with the change. It's happening with you or without you.

Business Perspective: Successful business organizations recognize that change is a vital and important dynamic for renewing and increasing profitability.

Seasons change. We are used to new growth in spring, full bloom in summer, falling leaves in autumn, cold bareness in winter. Nature has cycles of growth and decay. So why don't we embrace change as natural? Leaders can learn from their own and others' differing attitudes to change.

There is a natural process of growth and decay. It may be personal: primary, secondary, perhaps tertiary education. It may span centuries, as in the rise and fall of civilizations. We see it in relationships: slow beginnings, healthy development, realizing it is time to move on.

Change does not happen in isolation. A local church may be at one stage of its evolution while its surrounding community is at another. Church leaders and members may be at different stages in their personal and professional lives. We need to recognize each other's situation.

How do we respond to change? We have different needs: everyone is on a spectrum between preferring stability and exploration. Helping everyone to be aware of such preferences in themselves and one another is a crucial role for a leader. Exploratory people may get frustrated at those preferring stability; the latter may be irritated by endless innovation from the former.

The period between the top of one change curve and the bottom of another can be uncertain and turbulent. Leaders have a crucial role to play in promoting security, especially through relentless consistency of approach. But where do we find our security?

The scriptures abound with confidence in God (Psalm 27.2 Corinthians 5, for example). As humans, each of us is on a spectrum between finding security through people and through an idea or symbol. For some this may the security of the Book of Common Prayer or other liturgies. For others it will be through spiritual social gatherings such as New Wine, Soul Survivor or Walsingham.

We are all somewhere on these exploration and security spectrums. Different attitudes are attracted to different stages of the change curve, but work best when balanced. We need solid points of security and we need new ideas. Such diversity is natural and should be welcomed as a sign of health.

Recognizing the change process as part of the leadership of a church can serve as a dynamic framework for proposed changes. Such an overview can enable the church leader to be aware of their own and other people's exploration and security preferences. It is essential that those charged with overseeing change in the church recognize their own role in providing security in times of uncertainty.

Consistency through the process combined with openness and transparency is vital.

For reflection and discussion

1 Do you have the capacity to recognize where you are in the change process?
2 What is the current attitude to change in your church? (In this discussion try to identify the 'sacred cows': are they healthy or unhealthy?)
3 Use some examples of well-known non-church-related events that demonstrate how change had led to positive outcomes. Now construct a model for your own church working backwards from now.
4 Construct another model for change that looks forward in the life of your church and discuss the possible outcomes, fears and hopes.

Great Idea 42

Embrace Failure

RICHARD YOUNG

Embrace failure! Encourage your congregations to experiment with new ideas to develop the church's life and mission. Before they try something new, discuss openly the main things that could go wrong. Only go ahead if you all agree that even if the experiment 'failed' it would still have been worth trying – and so free them from the paralysing fear of getting things wrong.

Great Idea 43

Embrace the Social Media

A Case Study

PETER COLWELL

Churches Together in Britain and Ireland, and its predecessor the British Council of Churches, is an ecumenical organization that seeks to serve the churches of Britain and Ireland in their journey towards Christian unity.

During 2009 CTBI took a bold step in moving away from its previous modus operandi, which had hitherto involved a large office-based staff, to a new and more flexible way of working. This involved a smaller staff, most of whom work remotely, supported by a small office 'hub'. This smaller team makes full use of the range of online communication such as skype, video conferencing and social media to enhance and complement existing and more traditional forms of working such as face-to-face meetings.

Although this was in part a recognition of financial realities that almost all organizations in the charitable sector face, it also responded to a world that is more relational in its approach and which seeks to respond quickly to rapidly changing events and circumstances. In this changing world, the challenge is to continue to be innovative while not losing sight of the goals of the organization and the need to deliver a product that at least matches the high standards of the past.

A growing element to this new way of working is the use of tools such as Facebook and Twitter that help to share with a wider constituency the work of CTBI. However another element of this strategy has been the development of Churches Together Connect which is the interactive home of Churches Together.

This makes use of the social networking approach in providing a platform for individuals involved in the ecumenical movement in Britain and Ireland to share insights, news and to engage in wider discussion and reflection. With a range of discussion forums and blogs, as well as 'closed' space for existing ecumenical groups, networks and forums, there is the opportunity to explore particular issues in more detail through the virtual world.

Recent issues that have been explored because of this new media include:

- Is Interfaith the New Ecumenism?
- How do you engage in ministry and mission in a digital age?
- Israel–Palestine – what is the way forward?
- Celebrating 400 years of the King James Bible

Alongside these social media developments, CTBI has also offered free websites for local Churches Together groups which provide a ready-made but adaptable website that can be populated by local information but also provides automatic 'feeds' from CTBI and the National Ecumenical Instruments in England, Ireland, Scotland and Wales which not only enables the website to be kept fresh with new material but also means that ecumenical developments nationally can be more quickly received and understood locally.

Potentially this enables local groups to communicate more quickly with national ecumenical organizations and also with each other through CT Connect; sharing ideas, initiatives and best practice.

One of the earliest criticisms of CTBI's embracing of this new strategy was 'I hope they are not doing this simply because they can'. The real danger with social media is that the medium does indeed become the message and that content is sacrificed in favour of presentation. CTBI has been clear that its vision remains firmly rooted in the prayer of Jesus – that the disciples might be one that the world might believe.

Embracing the various aspects of social media and digital engagement means that rather than moving away from 'content', the ecumenical movement in the twenty-first century is able to refresh its vision and better explore what it means for the church and all Christians to be one.

For reflection and discussion

1 What was the business case for CTBI to move to online working?
2 What do you think will be the future business benefits for CTBI in moving to online working?

Great Idea 44

Enable Effective Partnering
Worksheet

RICHARD FOX

The purpose of this worksheet is to provide you with a checklist to enable you to evaluate the efficacy of partner working. Please photocopy the worksheet for use with your groups.

A feature of church working has always been partner working and in today's environment its significance is taking on greater importance. Such alliances can add value to meeting customer needs and growing the church. Many organizations within the public and private sector also understand the importance of partnering as part of their business portfolio. This method of working can form as much as 60 to 80 per cent of their leadership and management style of working.

Effective leadership and management of partnering arrangements can result in, for example, the church being able to reach more people or share costs.

This checklist will enable you to evaluate existing partnership arrangements and provide a productive compact for future partner working.

Do you fully understand and have you quantified the market opportunity and the value for both partners and ultimately for the customer?	Yes	No
Do you have the competencies to shift mindsets from supplier–customer to a collaborative culture?	Yes	No
Do you have the competencies to build trust and credibility quickly?	Yes	No
Do you have the competencies to create and implement a management plan to influence others?	Yes	No
Can you build with your partner a shared vision and business objectives that are understood by staff in both organizations?	Yes	No
Can you jointly develop a set of performance metrics and institute joint monitoring?	Yes	No
Can you develop and share an understanding of what win-win-win will look like for the partners and importantly the customer?	Yes	No
Do you have access to professional legal advice?	Yes	No
Can you establish who will be the sponsor of the partnership working within each organization and do they have the authority to act?	Yes	No
Can you recognize and manage any cultural differences within the partners?	Yes	No
Do you have the competencies to manage changing expectations within the life of the partnership and can you revitalize, if necessary, long-established partnerships?	Yes	No
Have you in place mechanisms for knowledge exchange and sharing ideas for new services or products?	Yes	No
Have you in place arrangements for evaluating the productivity of the partnership and mechanisms for dealing with difficulties?	Yes	No
Have you in place arrangements for regularly evaluating the financial viability of the partners?	Yes	No

Great Idea 45

Engage in Radical Surgery

GREG HASLAM

> My Father is the gardener; he cuts off every branch
> that does not bear fruit
> John 15.1–2
>
> **Top Tip:** Healthy churches are the ambassadors of Christ in the outposts of the kingdom!
>
> **Business Perspective:** Successful commercial businesses understand that to remain profitable it is often necessary to engage in radical reorganization and restructuring. This requires managers who are prepared to be brave, unpopular but true to the mission of their organization.

The Church of Jesus Christ is beyond question God's greatest idea. The entrance of sin into the world disordered everything. It warped humanity, strained relationships, fragmented community, and robbed humankind of hope.

The gospel is the remedy and the Church is God's shopfront window of what he offers freely to all. His vision is to bring all things in heaven and earth together under one head, Jesus Christ.

Many believe that salvation is a human achievement, or at least a joint effort with God in which we play a major part. Actually, we contribute nothing to our salvation but the sin we need to be saved from. Paul credits our rescue entirely to God through Jesus who is central to this recovery.

The result is a new humanity, a new community, a 'glorious church' intimately related and reconciled to God and one another through Jesus Christ and empowered by his Holy Spirit. We who are Christians are part of this new community.

If you understand this you will never settle for a warped or unhealthy church.

Healthy churches consist of:

1 Christ's ambassadors gathered under his kingship as outposts of heaven.
2 Those with managerial and spiritual 'clout' to effect change in individuals, communities, cities and nations.
3 God's supernatural energy which through us can accomplish astonishing things.
4 The capacity to counter the effects of sin and rebellion.
5 Visible evidence of God's power which is hard to explain and even harder to explain away.

An unhealthy church is one where Jesus is excluded and where other hands are often at the helm, not his. Leaders must decide who is boss and yield to him. Managing God's church is about resolving to do anything the Lord asks in order to turn things around before the disease becomes terminal.

This entails fearlessly making the gospel central to everything the church offers and does. This requires a boldness to preach and act upon all that God says to effect reform and renewal.

Radical surgery in the management of the church is needed for complete recovery. Radical surgery involves submission to both God's Word and Spirit so that Christ's voice is heard and change is here to stay. Such obedience may prove costly, but it won't be half as expensive as disobedience.

For reflection and discussion

1 How do you assess if your church is healthy?
2 What skills and competencies do you require to be a radical manager of your church?
3 How can you sustain and create ambassadors for your church?
4 What do you understand by managerial and spiritual clout?

Great Idea 46

Engage Openly with Disagreement

COLIN PATTERSON

> Everyone should be quick to listen,
> slow to speak and slow to anger
> James 1.19

Top Tip: Engage openly with disagreement and you'll usually lower, rather than raise, the level of tension.

Business Perspective: Successful organizations understand that maximizing the potential of their workforce means tapping into their creative and organizational knowledge. By such processes profitability and output is increased but requires an approach to management that embraces listening and reflection even when this involves conflict and disagreement.

There are numerous times in the New Testament and in church history which demonstrate that disagreement has been a catalyst for growth and transformation. Such times bring forth leaders who can move beyond defending self or traditions. Openness is their hallmark. Such leaders demonstrate an openness and a willingness to engage with those who hold contrary views and to learn from them.

Open engagement is more of a stance than a skill, but it points to certain habits worth cultivating. Here are five to work at:

Inviting expressions of disagreement

This is more than just biting your tongue when you long to answer back. It's saying things like, 'Who has a different perspective from what we've heard so far? Let's hear from them.'

Moving towards resistance

When someone disagrees with you strongly, your gut reaction might be to change the subject, or back off to prepare a counter-attack, or hold your cards close to your chest. But don't stop there. Try opening up a channel of further communication: 'I'm interested to explore what you've just said. Say a bit more to help me understand your concerns.'

Listening deeply

When you're thinking, 'There's no value in what this person is saying', stay open to revising your verdict. Aim to ponder actively: 'Have I understood what this is really about? Is there a different angle to consider? A wake-up call that I need to heed?' You can check that you're clear about what the other person is saying by offering a summary of it in your own words.

Grasping nettles

Sometimes a matter can rest once everyone has had their say. But often more is needed. So judge carefully the moments to stay engaged: 'Here's an issue that needs to be faced rather than buried. Let's stick with it. How might we address the various concerns that we've heard expressed? Is there a creative way forward?'

Being confrontable

But what about when you as the leader are part of the problem? Sometimes you are in the wrong, yet unable to see why, without the help of others. Maybe you have behaved in an unhelpful or hurtful way even if unintentionally and they are reluctant to draw it to your attention. You need to have an open-door mentality which enables you to seek and accept feedback from others. You can say, 'This is not easy for me to hear but I will think carefully about what you have said to me.' Paradoxically, being ready to hear hard things, even from the person who says them harshly, will often reduce the sense of pressure.

For reflection and discussion

1 Reflect on some recent incidents when you encountered disagreement.
2 To what extent were you displaying the five habits described above? Note your thoughts in a journal and discuss with your mentor or spiritual director.
3 Practise these habits, perhaps focusing on each for a couple of months.
4 Continue to reflect on specific incidents of disagreement. Review your journal and dialogue and celebrate any ways in which you can see that God has been at work.

Great Idea 47

Engage in the Power of Advertising

A Case Study

ROBERTA ROMINGER

There is a kairos moment for change. We prepare the way for it by steeping ourselves in the faith of Jesus. Then, whatever precipitates the moment (opportunity, crisis, conflict) we are ready to do something brave and right.

I will never forget the morning in December 2004 when I awoke to an email inbox filled with exciting messages from American friends. The United Church of Christ USA had just launched a television advert on the theme of the radical welcome of God in Christ.

> Jesus never turned anybody away. Neither do we. No matter who you are, or where you are on life's journey, you are welcome here.

The advertising was clever and edgy and it made the shivers run up my spine. But what was more thrilling to me was observing the transformation of my friends. They were proud of their church and excited about its exclusivity as an expression of the gospel. Over time they began to tell stories about all the media attention they were getting. More significantly, they told about contacts from people who had felt excluded by 'church' who wanted to know if the welcome was genuine. Watching this, I longed for something similar to happen to the URC.

A URC group went to visit the UCC in 2006 and came back full of enthusiasm. Exploratory meetings were held here in the UK. In 2008 we turned our enthusiasm into a proposal that the URC should enter into partnership with the UCC to become the first international expression of their campaign. This idea was approved by the Mission Council (our governing body) and funding was secured. But then there was a setback: copyright negotiations failed and the partnership had to be terminated. The URC was back on its own.

Through the early months of 2010 I travelled the length and breadth of the URC asking people, 'Tell me about a time when you felt most passionate or excited about something the URC had been or done or said.' I collected stories across a wonderful range of experiences but noticed that the theme of exclusivity featured in every conversation.

This confirmed the conviction already held by the steering group that we should seek to express the message of welcome for the British public as the UCC had done in the USA. We contracted an ad agency called This is Real Art (TiRA). We said that Radical Welcome was our theme and that our target audience was anybody who saw a church noticeboard proclaiming, 'All are welcome!' and knew that it didn't apply to them. TiRA produced attention-grabbing headlines and amazing artwork, teaching us that the 'look' of the ads would be as important as the words in communicating our message.

In 2011 it was time to show the campaign to the churches and invite them to embark on the preparations that would enable them to them to advertise Radical Welcome with integrity and confidence. Bible study sits alongside practical exercises in the training materials.

In a denomination that is naturally suspicious of anything that comes from the 'centre', there has been some controversy. However, the campaign has already been successful, in that over 350 churches are now actively engaging with the challenge of Radical Welcome, which will surely be transformative.

Great Idea 48

Establish a Lay-led Church Plant

A Case Study

DARRELL GARDINER

For ten years at Easter, Harvest and Christmas, members of Holy Trinity Anglican Church, Formby, invited residents of the Alt Road Estate to attend church assuring them of a warm welcome.

Disappointingly, very few responded and by 1991 after so many endeavours it was only too clear that of the 1,150 homes on the estate only 40 had formed any kind of link with Holy Trinity. The geography of the neighbourhood tends to mitigate against outreach: it is remotely situated from Holy Trinity, its parish church, and it is surrounded by busy major roads.

With the Decade of Evangelism gathering momentum, it was time for fresh thinking, a new approach, and no idea seemed better than the prospect of planting a church convenient for residents within a few minutes of their homes.

Redgate County Primary School was centrally located and directly opposite the shopping parade. It was not just the obvious place to plant a church, it was the only place likely to be suitable.

The Vicar of Holy Trinity appointed a licensed lay reader to explore possibilities and enquiries began. The school governors were pleased to offer a hall with coffee bar facilities, a music room and a library at £40 for a two-hour period.

A team of 25 was formed as an 'instant' congregation with the skills of musical talent, ability to lead prayers and read lessons, the skills to convert the hall into a worship centre, and the commitment to leave the premises as they found it.

Mission has always been a strategic objective for leadership of Holy Trinity and they pledged financial support for the first year.

With everything in place approval was sought from the Diocese of Liverpool.

Unexpectedly the school governors disclosed that there was competition for the use of its premises and requested Holy Trinity to begin Sunday worship without delay otherwise they would lose the facility. Consequently all thoughts of training the team disappeared, together with the prospects of learning visits to other existing church plants.

In the meantime the diocese gave its blessing so posters were displayed, a welcome card delivered to each home on the estate, local press notices released and 25 lay people were commissioned at an early Holy Communion and were on their way across the parish to introduce Holy Trinity Redgate's opening service of worship.

Untrained but ready, they began. There was uncertainty, but there was hope and faith and most certainly love. Eighty-seven new people came to this first service, a level of attendance which has been sustained.

The original team has now withdrawn and handed over their tasks to local residents under the pastoral care of the licensed lay reader from Holy Trinity.

The ingredients for the success stemmed from a fresh approach to worship that was easily understood and accessible to a previously non-church community. The worship focused on the spiritual needs and well-being of that community rather than a tradition of worship that was not part of their experience.

For reflection and discussion

1 What was the business case for Holy Trinity establishing a church plant?
2 What do you think will be the future business benefits for Holy Trinity in establishing the church plant?

Great Idea 49

Expand the Community

JOLYON EDWARDES

To expand any community effectively it is important to understand what that community needs. Asking this question of your community creates active participation and generates loyalty and participation. Congregations are not passive unless you make them so.

Great Idea 50

Expect the Unexpected

MICHAEL LOFTHOUSE

> If the owner of the house had known at what hour the thief was coming he would not have let his house be broken into
> Luke 12.39
>
> **Top Tip:** Remember it is not if but when the next screw-up hits.
>
> **Business Perspective:** A successful organization understands that it is essential to prepare businesses and institutions so as to be able to respond and recover from different threats that could produce losses to business and prevent business resumption. It is no longer enough to think of business as normal day-to-day activities claiming that nothing could happen which will impact on our profitability or that we will not be affected like others.

A certainty of management is that no matter how much energy you expend on managing and leading, planning and strategizing, someone or something will screw it all up.

Faced with the increased complexity that surrounds the management of the modern church you should expect an external force or more likely an internal member of the congregation to create a crisis that impacts on your ability to function normally. It is managerially insufficient to believe that there are no events that will significantly stop or inhibit your daily work.

In the commercial world this reality is acknowledged and managed through a process called Business Continuity Management. There is even a corresponding British Standard, BSI 25999-1-2. It can be defined as: the management discipline of identifying vulnerabilities and risks, and planning in advance how to mitigate, accept, or assign them in event of a business disruption.

In practice have you planned for and are able to avoid or mitigate risks? Can you reduce the impact of a crisis? Can you reduce the time it takes to restore conditions to a state of business as usual?

It is not a difficult task to sit down and work out what may disrupt your daily operations. Of course some of these disruptions may not be significant enough to turn into a crisis but others may be. For example, if the lead gets stripped off your church roof, despite your very best efforts to prevent it, where will you hold services? Often we only think of infrastructure, but people are just as significant. Who will replace that one person who is leading the church plant project?

For the church, crises that centre on people are often more significant than infrastructure. You can always move to the church hall or local school to hold services. Remember business continuity management strives to keep you operating at levels that existed before the crisis struck. The whole object is not to let anybody down. Your reputation is also at stake. Contemporary ideas about accountability mean you are more responsible for deficiencies.

Follow this three-step process.

1 Identify the major risks that may interrupt business as usual. These are called the critical business processes. Not every interruption and not every function is critical. This is largely an intuitive process; you know what must continue and what you can allow to slip.
2 Develop a plan with the key members of your congregation to mitigate or reduce the impact. Common sense has a large part to play in business continuity management at this level.
3 Communicate and if possible test the plan. Remember it could be you that prompts the crisis and you might not be around to put the plan into action.

Remember it is not if but when the next screw-up hits.

For reflection and discussion

1 What contingency plans do you currently have in place in your church?
2 If your church became unavailable for worship what would you do?
3 What would you most like to do in your church and community?
4 If you can do something radically different in a crisis can you do it now?

Great Idea 51

Explore the Skills You Need

LEN COLLINSON

> A person of knowledge uses words with restraint
> Proverbs 17.27
>
> **Top Tip:** Preach the gospel, whichever way you can, if necessary use words.
>
> **Business Perspective:** Some managerial approaches can be best expressed diagramatically thereby demonstrating internal relationships between the different functions in the management and leadership process.

The diagrams that follow offer an explanation of three tools that will be of vital and immense value to any church leader or management group (see Figures 3, 4 and 5).

Study the diagrams carefully and make notes as you interpret them. You can do this as a group exercise then share the notes you have made.

Discussion Groups for exploration and action

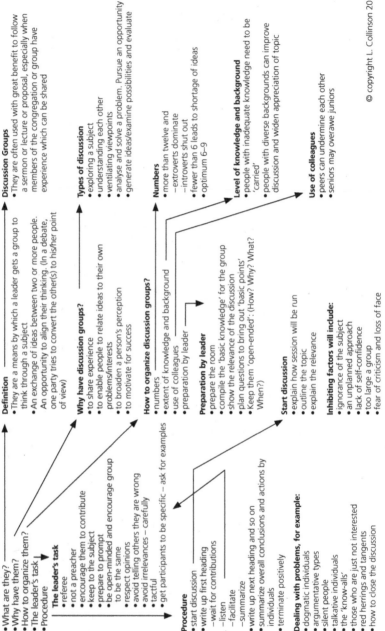

- What are they?
- Why have them?
- How to organize them?
- The leader's task
- Procedure

Definition
- They are a means by which a leader gets a group to think through a subject
- An exchange of ideas between two or more people. (In a debate, one party tries to convert the other(s) to his/her point of view)

Discussion Groups
- They are often used with great benefit to follow a sermon or lecture or proposal, especially when members of the congregation or group have experience which can be shared

The leader's task
- referee
- not a preacher
- encourage them to contribute
- keep to the subject
- prepare to prompt
- be open-minded and encourage group to be the same
- respect opinions
- avoid telling others they are wrong
- avoid irrelevances – carefully
- tactful
- get participants to be specific – ask for examples

Why have discussion groups?
- to share experience
- to enable people to relate ideas to their own problems/interests
- to broaden a person's perception
- to motivate for success

Types of discussion
- exploring a subject
- understanding each other
- ventilating viewpoints
- analyse and solve a problem. Pursue an opportunity
- generate ideas/examine possibilities and evaluate

How to organize discussion groups?
- numbers
- extent of knowledge and background
- use of colleagues
- preparation by leader

Numbers
- more than twelve and
  - extroverts dominate
  - introverts shut out
- fewer than 6 leads to shortage of ideas
- optimum 6-9

Preparation by leader
- prepare the room
- compile the 'basic knowledge' for the group
- show the relevance of the discussion
- plan questions to bring out 'basic points'
- Keep them 'open-ended': (How? Why? What? When?)

Level of knowledge and background
- people with inadequate knowledge need to be 'carried'
- people with diverse backgrounds can improve discussion and widen appreciation of topic

Start discussion
- explain how session will be run
- outline the topic
- explain the relevance

Use of colleagues
- peers can undermine each other
- seniors may overawe juniors

Procedure
- start discussion
- write up first heading
  - wait for contributions
  - listen
  - facilitate
  - summarize
- write up next heading and so on
- summarize overall conclusions and actions by individuals
- terminate positively

Dealing with problems, for example:
- dogmatic individuals
- argumentative types
- silent people
- talkative individuals
- the 'know-alls'
- those who are just not interested
- red herrings and tangents
- how to close the discussion

Inhibiting factors will include:
- ignorance of the subject
- an unplanned approach
- lack of self-confidence
- too large a group
- fear of criticism and loss of face

Figure 3

120

Performance of groups and individuals

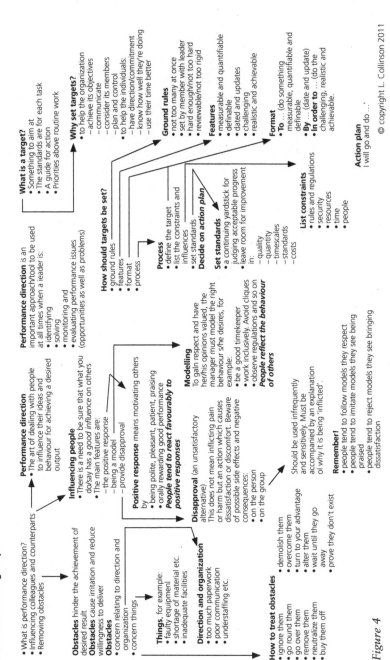

- What is performance direction?
- Influencing colleagues and counterparts
- Removing obstacles

Performance direction
- The art of dealing with people to influence their ideas and behaviour for achieving a desired output

Performance direction is an important approach/tool to be used at all times when a leader is:
- identifying
- solving
- monitoring and
- evaluating performance issues (opportunities as well as problems)

What is a target?
- Something to aim at
- The standards are for each task
- A guide for action
- Priorities above routine work

Why set targets?
- to help the organization
  - achieve its objectives
  - communicate
  - consider its members
  - plan and control
- to help the individuals:
  - have direction/commitment
  - know how well they're doing
  - use their time better

Obstacles hinder the achievement of desired result
Obstacles cause irritation and reduce willingness to deliver

Obstacles
- concern relating to direction and organization
- concern things

Influencing people
- There is a need to be sure that what you do/say has a *good influence* on others
- The main features are:
  - the positive response
  - being a model
  - provide disapproval

Positive response means motivating others by
- being polite, pleasant, patient, praising
- orally rewarding good performance
  People tend to react favourably to positive responses

Ground rules
- not too many at once
- set by member with leader
- hard enough/not too hard
- reviewable/not too rigid

Features
- measurable and quantifiable
- definable
- dated and updates
- challenging
- realistic and achievable

How should targets be set?
- ground rules
- features
- format
- process

Things, for example:
- faulty equipment
- shortage of material etc.
- inadequate facilities

Direction and organization
- too much paperwork
- poor communication
- understaffing etc.

Modelling
To gain respect and have her/his opinions valued, the manager must model the right behaviour s/he desires, for example:
- be a good timekeeper
- work inclusively. Avoid cliques
- observe regulations and so on
  People reflect the behaviour of others

Process
- define the target
- list the constraints and influences
- set standards
- **Decide on action plan**

Set standards
- a continuing yardstick for judging acceptable progress
- leave room for improvement in:
  - quality
  - quantity
  - timescales
  - standards
  - costs

List constraints
- rules and regulations
- security
- resources
- time
- people

Disapproval (an unsatisfactory alternative)
This does not mean inflicting pain or harm but an action which causes dissatisfaction or discomfort. Beware of possible side effects and negative consequences:
- on the person
- on the group

Should be used infrequently and sensitively. Must be accompanied by an explanation ol of why it is being 'inflicted'.

Format
- **To** ... (do something measurable, quantifiable and definable
- **By** ... (date and update)
- **In order to** ... (do the challenging, realistic and achievable.

Remember!
- people tend to follow models they respect
- people tend to imitate models they see being praised
- people tend to reject models they see bringing dissatisfaction

How to treat obstacles
- ignore them
- go round them
- go over them
- remove them
- neutralize them
- buy them off
- demolish them
- overcome them
- turn to your advantage
- alter them
- wait until they go away
- prove they don't exist

Action plan
I will go and do ...'

© copyright L. Collinson 2011

Figure 4

121

Completing Projects

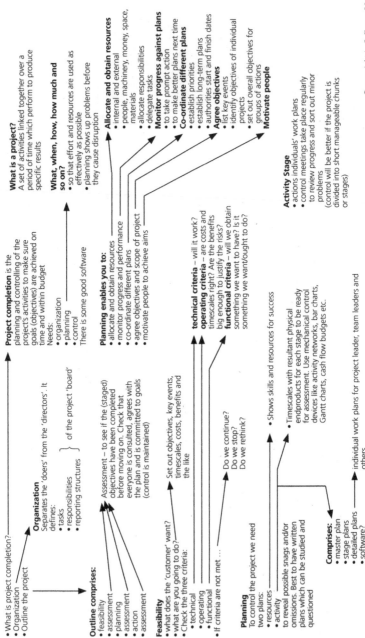

- What is project completion?
- Organization
- Outline the project

What is a project?
A set of activities linked together over a period of time which perform to produce specific results

What, when, how, how much and so on?
- so that effort and resources are used as effectively as possible
- planning shows up problems before they cause disruption

Allocate and obtain resources
- internal and external
- people, machinery, money, space, materials
- allocate responsibilities
- delegate tasks

Monitor progress against plans
- to take prompt action
- to make better plans next time

Co-ordinate different plans
- authorities start and finish dates

Agree objectives
- establish priorities
- establish long-term plans
- list key events
- identify objectives of individual projects
- set out overall objectives for groups of actions

Motivate people

Project completion is the planning and controlling of the project's activities to make sure goals (objectives) are achieved on time and within budget
Needs:
- organization
- planning
- control
There is some good software

Planning enables you to:
- allocate and obtain resources
- monitor progress and performance
- co-ordinate different plans
- agree objectives and scope of project
- motivate people to achieve aims

technical criteria – will it work?
operating criteria – are costs and timescales right? Are the benefits big enough to justify the risks?
functional criteria – will we obtain something we want to have? Is it something we want/ought to do?

Activity Stage
- actions individuals' work plans
- control meetings take place regularly to review progress and sort out minor problems
(control will be better if the project is divided into short manageable chunks or stages)

Organization
Separates the 'doers' from the 'directors'. It defines:
- tasks
- responsibilities   } of the project 'board'
- reporting structures

Outline comprises:
- feasibility
- assessment
- planning
- assessment
- action
- assessment

Assessment – to see if the (staged) objectives have been completed before moving on. Check that everyone is consulted, agrees with the plan and is committed to goals (control is maintained)

Feasibility
- what does the 'customer' want?
- what are you going to do?
- Check the three criteria:
- technical
- operating
- functional
- If criteria are not met …

Do we continue?
Do we stop?
Do we rethink?

Set out objectives, key events, timescales, costs, benefits and the like

- Shows skills and resources for success

- Timescales with resultant physical endproducts for each stage to be ready for assessment. Use mechanical control devices like activity networks, bar charts, Gantt charts, cash flow budgets etc.

Planning
To control the project we need two plans:
- resources
- activity
to reveal possible snags and/or omissions. Best to have written plans which can be studied and questioned

Comprises:
- master plan
- stage plans
- detailed plans
- software?

individual work plans for project leader, team leaders and others

Figure 5

122

For reflection and discussion

1 What are discussion groups?
   Why have them?
   How can they be organized?
   What is the leader's task and what are their procedures?
2 Performance of groups and individuals
   What is performance direction?
   What influences colleagues and counterparts?
   How do we remove obstacles?
3 Completing projects
   What is project completion?
   What does the organization of a project entail?
   What does a project outline look like?

Great Idea 52

Fill Your Leadership Space

HUGH MARTYN

The spirit of the Lord is on me because he has anointed me to
preach good news to the poor
Luke 4.18

Top Tip: If you do not fill your leadership space voids appear, and
in voids bad things happen.

Business Perspective: Successful commercial organizations
invest time and money in the development of their leaders. They
understand that leadership is a developmental process and that
good leaders will increase profitability.

If we consider that each leader fills a space within the organization in terms of role and responsibility, how do we allow individuals to self-reflect and assess whether they fill their place in the
overall organizational space?

Poor leadership is experienced when the leader fails to fill the
space occupied in role and context, and good leadership is evident
when the individual fills the role and environment they occupy.

Failure to fill your leadership space will create voids and in
those voids bad things will happen; discrimination, harassment,
bullying, poor performance, and failure to protect the public.

The key question is how do we measure or assess this? An obvious question, yet it fails to grasp the issue that filling your leadership space is not just doing things right or doing the right thing, it
is to increase the leadership capacity of the organization to a level
that will enhance its performance and reputation.

Where management is designed to preserve the status quo, it traps leaders within a particularly narrow range of leadership options. When so trapped, to make sense of the interactions of their organization and its environment, it may be argued that leaders adopt an empiricist approach based on organizational and personal experience. Therefore leaders become a prisoner of the social, political and economic context.

Can a leadership philosophy exist that allows its leadership any predictive certainty? Much leadership literature treats leaders as free agents, unfettered, not recognizing the importance of the bureaucracy, governance and structural constraints of an organization.

When we bury leadership in a superabundance of attributes leadership competencies can only be achieved at the cost of individuals losing their ability to act individually, reinforcing homogeneity of leadership.

The proposition of measuring leadership space is not seen as a performance management activity but rather as a development tool for leaders to gain the necessary awareness as to their knowledge and skills for effective performance. The organization may then be in a position to consider that the leader is working competently to fill the space within the organization in terms of role and responsibility.

If we allow individuals to self-reflect and assess whether they have the clarity of purpose, competence and passion to achieve, they will seek to grow and expand their leadership capacity.

Consequently leaders can transcend their role leading to an enhanced reputation. Ultimately their leadership is realized in the organization and the communities they serve.

Importantly for this cognitive leadership model to hold value for the individual they need to have the necessary personal integrity and humility to reflect honestly, the personal awareness to seek out if 'voids' exist in their leadership, and passion for achievement in the will to increase their leadership capacity to fill the leadership space they occupy. Or maybe more importantly, to seek out if their people's leadership fills the space they occupy.

For reflection and discussion

1 How do you define your leadership space?
2 How do you support your leadership development that allows you to develop and transcend your role?
3 What is it that you require from your organization to enable you to become an effective leader?
4 How do I know when other people fill my leadership space?

Great Idea 53

Form a Messy Church

A Case Study

KATH ROGERS

As with many parishes we had housing estates with many families but few worshipping despite our church plant established 19 years ago in a local primary school. Locally there are thriving Sunday football leagues and shops and coffee bars are busy on Sunday mornings. Formby reflects wider disparate society.

A fresh expression of church was needed to reach these families; we had to go out and meet people where they were and at times and places convenient for them, as Sunday morning in a Victorian church, or even in a local school, was obviously not.

Following visits to local Messy Churches we identified a local community centre and a local state school as good central and neutral locations for the two estates. We partnered with our neighbouring parish and obtained the support of Churches Together in Formby, Altcar and Hightown. A young team of predominantly lay members of our two churches enabled Messy Church Formby to happen and extensive publicity through the local schools, leafleting of estates and the press allowed its launch on Pentecost 2010.

We have just celebrated our second birthday and have settled into a monthly pattern of worship alternately at each venue repeating the theme of the event. This year the themes have been: Who is God, Who is Jesus and Who is the Holy Spirit.

Messy Church begins with welcome and invitation for families to join in with a variety of crafts and games relating to the theme. There are usually eight to ten different crafts and games and this part of the church takes an hour. We then go to worship which is family friendly including action songs, prayer activities and some quiet reflection time. Finally we have a simple meal together and during that time give out notices and celebrate birthdays. Although Messy Church is a format, each church has its own atmosphere and takes time to establish itself as a worshipping community. The Messy Church in the school has quickly established itself as a community of faith with real friendships and fellowship over the meals.

We were anxious not to poach families from other churches, and we haven't. We have built up a regular congregation of families who find 'ordinary church' too difficult, and the majority of these are families on the fringe of the church from baptism contacts, toddler groups and church schools. Some of our families did not previously go to church and are very committed to Messy Church. Some families used to come to church but as children got older stopped coming on Sunday mornings but now enjoy Messy Church.

Each Messy Church has a turnover of new families; some of these stick and some don't. An unexpected area of growth arose from the need for a large number of volunteers. A number of teenagers have come on board and really enjoy leading the craft sessions and this has become their church. Each Messy Church has 60 to 85 people attending and of these approximately 25 to 35 are children, 30 are volunteers, and the remainder are the children's parents, grandparents and grown-up siblings. Approximately two-thirds of the volunteers usually worship on Sunday mornings.

If you are looking for growth in usual Sunday morning attendance then Messy Church does not work. It is not a 'half-way house'. It has integrity in its own right as a worshipping community. However if you want growth in faith, growth in learning about God, experience of fun, fellowship over a meal, and experience of God in worship, then Messy Church is a good strategy for growth. As a fresh expression of church it both reaches those families that traditional church services don't and it enables a growth in confidence and expression in the faith and commitment of the volunteers.

> **For reflection and discussion**
>
> 1 What was the business case for a Messy Church?
> 2 What do you think will be the future business benefits for the church in running a Messy Church?

Great Idea 54

Get Social with the Media

BEN PENNINGTON

A crowd came together in bewilderment because each one heard them declaring the wonders of God in their own language
Acts 2.6

Top Tip: Ensure your website has monitoring software like Google Analytic so that you can monitor how your website is being used by visitors.

Business Perspective: Successful organizations communicate with their customers in language and media that the customer uses and understands. Modern organizations understand and utilize every possible customer-focused means of communication to drive profitability.

Social networks such as LinkedIn, Twitter, Facebook and Flickr are already having a profound impact on the world. Twitter has enabled young rebels in North Africa and the Middle East to share frustrations and organize protests which have triggered the toppling of governments. Its beauty is its ease.

All you need is an internet connection or mobile phone and you can communicate to mass audiences immediately without the need for a newspaper, radio or television. In the business world these networks now play an expanding role in helping businesses communicate their products, services, messages and activities to their target audiences.

Churches and parishes can benefit from this technological revolution in helping to reach out to new people and nuture congregation members while promoting what they do. Jesus and his disciples were great communicators. In essence that is all social media is, a modern form of communication, a way of reaching people and involving them in the church community.

The Economist magazine has predicted that social media will enable a person in the 'new world' to maintain 500 friendships instead of the average 125 since the invention of the telephone. In less than the time it takes to buy a Christmas card you can send a message via social media to your entire social network.

For a parish the opportunity which modern social media offers is just too important and strategic to be ignored. At the present time the most effective media are LinkedIn, Facebook and Twitter. These are the main sites used in business.

Facebook is generally well known. Twitter is essentially a rolling newswire. Each tweet has to be no more than 140 characters or 20 words and can promote an event, a service or a piece of church news. It is wise to link as much back as you can to your church website so include a webpage link in the tweet. It is best to put this through http//tiny.cc/ a website which shortens weblinks and monitors the click through rate. For example a church may advertise as follows:

Annual Diocesan Pilgrimage to Lourdes end of July. Details and booking forms available at http//tiny.cc/697yo

A Twitter account is free and straightforward to do. It should be networked around other relevant organizations. Your church is then registered as a follower of that organization and they can follow you and see all your tweets.

LinkedIn is a more effective social networking site for parishes. Essentially it is for individuals. It is free and allows the user to build a profile like a CV. The user can then add Twitter feed to their profile so that all their tweets will be uploaded for contacts to see.

LinkedIn is enormously popular and many parishioners will be using it for business purposes. LinkedIn offers the opportunity to put the parish on the radar of the congregation during the week. The result is a parish life and profile beyond the Sunday service and into day-to-day life.

For reflection and discussion

1 How many in your church use the internet for communication?
2 How is the internet and social media perceived in your church community?
3 How might your church make use of its own website and social media pages?
4 How effective are your media communications?

Great Idea 55

God has Provided, now Manage it

DAVID CORNICK

There remains, I think, real confusion about the relationship between ministry, management and leadership, all of which are slippery and elastic words, but we can all benefit in our own ways from thinking that through in our varying contexts. But there is, still, unfortunately, belief that the necessary skills will descend from heaven that prevents such productive reflection.

Great Idea 56

Have a Biblical Vision

BEN REES

That the man of God may be complete,
thoroughly equipped for every good work
2 Timothy 3.17

Top Tip: Implementing the Bible will revolutionize the lives of
every disciple.

Business Perspective: All successful organizations create,
maintain and implement their operations manual. The operations
manual ensures that the organization is cost effective, the
potential of the workforce is maximized and that everyone in the
organization understands what they are doing and why.

The Bible tells us clearly, where there is no vision the people will
perish. In other words they will be unable to do their work as
passionately as they should and fail to fulfil their potential, as
God's witnesses. We can add to this biblical insight by stating,
where there are no biblical visions the Church of God has not fulfilled its goal of being a spiritual home to those who have received
God's call.

All the great leaders of the Christian faith have without excep-
tion been inspired by the biblical vision, for the Bible is the inspired
message of God. In the New Testament the apostle Paul tells us:
'All Scripture is given by inspiration of God, and is profitable for
doctrine, for reproof, for correction, for instruction in righteous-
ness (2 Timothy 3.16).

There is nothing more essential for the Church and its leaders than to study the biblical vision and to put into practice what the Gospels ask of us as peacemakers, people of prayer and praise, helpers of the afflicted and counsellors of hope and love.

If every church is to grow as a healthy church it should consider holding at least every three months a biblical 'Vision Day' with the purpose of inspiring the whole congregation. A biblically based vision conference should aim at inviting at least 60 participants so that it becomes a vehicle of grace and hope.

The purpose of such a day is to build the spiritual and missionary life of every member of the congregation. Here is a simple recipe for running your biblical Vision Day:

Invite someone who can lead your day and someone who can present a keynote address. Don't do this yourself, this day is for you as well.

Begin with an address on the importance of the Bible, its themes, its message of inspiration, and other relevant issues.

Have a coffee and chat break, with good coffee!

Introduce a competent and inspiring guest speaker or leader to speak about his or her own experience of mission and ministry and the importance of the Bible within that mission and ministry.

Have a lunch break of a good length with a good lunch!

After lunch offer two sessions of 50 minutes. The 60 people present should be divided into four groups of 15 participants under a committed Christian leader to discuss the morning session. A member of the group should be delegated to give a ten-minute résumé of what took place in the discussion group.

Complete the day with a summing-up plenary by the conference chairman who is able to spell out the vision for the church for the next three months.

Where the church has a number of families with children offer to run a programme to look after the children and young people. Invite an outside team to do this for you so that your own children and young people's leaders can benefit from this day.

If you do not have children and young people in your church then your Vision Day is already long overdue.

The Bible states clearly that true understanding of God's word understood in true fellowship can revolutionize the lives of every disciple of Jesus. We come to understand the meaning of being brothers and sisters in Christ. We come also to understand the meaning of a biblically based vision and are always prepared to give an encouraging answer to those who would like to join our Christian community

---

For reflection and discussion

1 How is the Bible used in your church?
2 What is the biblically based vision for your church at present?
3 What Bible passage do you think most speaks to your church at present?
4 How might a Bible Vision Day lead to healthy growth in your church?

Great Idea 57

Have a Metric for Rural Church Management

IAN TOMLINSON

> I am come that they might have life
> and that they might have it more abundantly
> John 10.10
>
> **Top Tip:** Metrics help simplify the difficult.
>
> **Business Perspective:** Successful organizations create and maintain appropriate measurement mechanisms to ensure that they are fulfilling their purpose profitably. Such metrics let the organization know when they are on or off track on a daily basis.

It can be beneficial to have a personal set of measures for day-to-day working. Here are my own which have proved managerially effective in 32 years of rural ministry:

1 Aim statement: 'Pray, Work, Read' – interpreting St Benedict's rule of life for today's world and in the parishioners' experience. 'He was Vicar of large things in a small parish' (R. S. Thomas) which is a reminder of the potential of my personal calling, tested by my experience of working with others.

2 Exploration of collaborative and complementary ways of working between clergy and laity, as each being members of the people of God, in finding, making and taking different roles for the sake of the task.

3 Searching for signs of God's kingdom in a lovely part of God's world with pockets of rural deprivation, alongside high levels of disposable income.

4 Annual review process in place, focused on the Annual Church Meeting, with SMART targets and SWOT analyses – 'Doing a few things and doing them well' – from Mission Shaped Church Audit. 'Succession Planning breeds success …'

5 Primary discipleship for Christians' vocations as being located in the world of responsible citizenship, as subjects of the kingdom of God, not hiding in the life of the church, escaping the demands of reality.

6 Priority of worship and keeping the same time for Sunday services with a team of worship leaders, lay and ordained with training.

7 Praying the parishes, ringing the bell regularly, waiting on the Spirit, realize the distinctive opportunities for numerically small, but vibrant congregations.

8 Getting the money in – not by moralizing at people but by meeting our church household budgeting practically and responsibly by giving away to missions and charities, as part of an annual round of planned giving.

9 Making all church meetings eucharistic in the sense of celebration and times of thanksgiving. A job worth doing and doing well, while having fun.

10 Delegation of essential tasks to individuals and working parties of parishioners and reporting back of achievements to the Parochial Church Councils, signing them off and moving forward.

11 Giving due attention to holding ideas in the mind (two sides of the same coin) – institution: sacraments, Scripture, spirituality, etc., needing leadership; organization: finance, fabric, administration, etc., requiring management.

12 Importance of community emphasis and rhythm. Community use of parish church public spaces. Liturgical year as a resource.

13 Lavatories and kitchens installed.

14 Benefice ministry team, with input from diocese and deanery, with discernment, recruitment and development of potential leaders.
15 Thinking in decades for planning major development.
16 Not romanticizing rural living – realistic understanding of agricultural issues and pressures and celebrating God in creation.
17 Delivery of regular newsletter to every house in the benefice with church and community news and list of services and contact with clergy and other representative people, such as churchwardens.
18 Weekly contact with and support of village schools. Networking of all-age worship opportunities with invitations sent out.
19 Pattern of study groups, as appropriate.
20 Attending to unconscious processes in individuals, groups and organizations, as a resource to access the divine in the human.
21 Being reliably available, using modern technology, for example websites, telephone answering system, emails, etc. (including, for example, conference calls with busy churchwardens to expedite business).
22 Benefice administrative system and administrator in place.
23 Village pastoral care network acknowledged and accessed, rather than set up parallel church system.
24 Recognize and encourage the involvement of congregation in village associations, such as parish councils and other groups.
25 Use of the occasional offices of the Church – baptisms, marriages, funerals and other pastoral liturgies, for example healing, times of transition, etc.
26 Listening to unsolicited feedback as a golden resource to access what might be going on in the environment.
27 Care of bereaved by looking after churchyards and cemeteries to a very high standard.
28 Personal and professional development for the incumbent is vital.

For reflection and discussion

1 Which of the above relate to your own work situation and why?
2 Which do you consider unworkable and why?
3 Having reflected on this list, create your own daily working metric.
4 Share this metric with your leadership group and pray.

Great Idea 58

Have an Ethical Propaganda

MICHAEL LOFTHOUSE

> See what large letters I use as I write to you with my own hand!
> Galatians 6.11
>
> **Top Tip:** Public relations messages must support the strategic intention of the church and be designed to be digestible by the target audience.
>
> **Business Perspective:** Successful commercial organizations realize that you are only as good as your image. It is profitable to devote resources to the building and sustaining of your image through professional and sustained public relations activities.

There is no room for painful amateurism in the fiercely competitive environments that surround local churches. St Paul understood this maxim. A prolific practitioner of public relations it was he who crystallized a burgeoning religious cult into a world religion. Paul used speeches, letters, staged events and public relations interventions to engage, attract and sustain customers.

The result was the establishment of new churches in the face of sustained opposition which have stood the test of time. He was an exemplar of the public relations practitioner, strategist, manager, customer relations expert and writer. He is the signpost to what the modern church requires, an effective bridge and credible spokesperson.

Paul understood the need for strategic underpinning of any public relations activities. Vision, intention and motive must be

141

clarified before engagement. Strategically churches are organizations with a product to sell and an image to sustain, existing in an often hostile and competitive market. Public relations is not negotiation, it is ethical propaganda; a tool for success, a vital managerial activity that contributes to profitability. Paul's public relations activities were religious in intent but also managerial; sustainable growth was the objective.

Paul also knew how to segment his customers. To be effective, public relations messages must support the strategic intention of the church and be designed to be digestible by the target audience. It could be argued that for Paul segmentation was simple, Gentiles and Jews. For the modern church public relations practitioner the segmentation has, in line with society, atomized into almost limitless customers. Understanding this fragmentation and not being overwhelmed by its complexity is the challenge.

So as not to be overwhelmed, a working model of public relations would recognize that there are now four broad segments of church customers.

1   Those strongly opposed to the church message.
2   Those unfamiliar with the church message.
3   Those aware of but ambivalent to the church message.
4   Those aware and who actively participate.

Segmentation may need to be further subdivided by other criteria, such as age, to ensure that your message is understood by the target audience. Such disaggregation enables managerial intervention. Can we do it? Will it be profitable? Is this our target audience? Is this the right message carried in the right medium? Remember PR recipients are also potential and current customers.

Given the limited resources of the local church, segmentation also allows you to target your public relations activities on the most profitable audience. For example the parish magazine may not reach the 18 year old in Segment 2 but Facebook or Twitter may.

Paul's public relations activities galvanized disparate, quarrelsome and often violent sects into an enduring world religion. The challenge for the modern church public relations practitioner is not as daunting but locally could be as significant as Paul's endeavours. Paul clearly had a PR toolkit to call upon, from his epistles to his rhetorical proficiency. Your managerial challenge is to create and sustain your own. Here is a starting point.

Create a workable infrastructure

A danger is in thinking that PR is located in such things as parish magazines or formal media such as newspapers and television. While not underestimating their importance, one of your most powerful PR tools is your infrastructure. Does your church and its associated buildings and environment support your strategic intention, mission and desired image? Is it customer friendly? View your church from the perspective of a potential customer. Is it visually attractive, is it customer friendly? Have you trained your churchwardens as 'greeters'. When did you last check your noticeboard? Does it match the visual effect of the competitors? Most churches occupy strategic important positions in their communities. Are you maximizing the frontage? It is your shop window.

Make links with local media

Is your parish magazine promoting your church? Evaluate it against other similar publications. Importantly, does your magazine grow and sustain your church? What working relationships do you have with your local newspapers and radio stations? How many stories have you had accepted in the past year? For example, when your linked mission partner visited did you generate a story? And remember, the newspapers are more likely to accept your story if it is accompanied by pictures.

Make use of social media

Electronic media provides complete editorial control. It is also cost effective. Here, you are the journalist. Your mobile phone is the television camera and YouTube your TV channel. Your website your newspaper and feature magazine. Twitter your 24-hour news channel. How many do you use?

Paul understood the importance of constructing the right message, using the right medium for the targeted audience. His skilful and persistent communication endeavours significantly contributed to the establishment of Christianity.

For reflection and discussion

1 What do you understand by effective public relations?
2 What part does social media such as Twitter and Facebook play in your current public relations strategy?
3 How do you measure the success of your public relations activities?
4 How do you get independent feedback on your public relations activities?

Great Idea 59

Hold Mid-week Meetings

PHILIP PLYMING

A time is coming and has now come when true worshippers
will worship the Father in spirit and truth
John 4.23

Top Tip: Sunday can be any day of the week.

Business Perspective: Successful organizations engage in market
research so that they can understand their customers and their
needs in order to deliver appropriate products. Customers will
always buy the products that they want and pass by the ones that
they don't.

Mid-week meetings can be very effective vehicles for growth for
those around during the day (often older people and families with
young children). In particular, they provide a low-key entry point
for people to experience something of Christian welcome and
fellowship, and hear something about Jesus Christ. Often this is
the first step to attending Sunday worship or doing a course such
as Alpha.

However, mid-week meetings are not effective by accident. In
order for them not to turn into clubs for the initiated, you need to
be intentional about making them a vehicle for mission. Here are
some key tips for effective mid-week meetings:

1   Be targeted: Who is this mid-week meeting for? There is little
    point in putting on a coffee morning and then expecting new
    people to come to it. Mixed-age events can work well for

established church members, but newcomers want to know that this event is for them. So, be clear who you hope to come to the event: mums and toddlers, older people, and then design the event around those people.

2 Be a team: Mid-week outreach meetings cannot be led by one person. They need a team of people who share a vision for outreach, who have a gift of welcoming and including people, and who pray regularly with and for each other and the ministry. Take time to assemble the right people in this team, and meet together four or five times to pray about the ministry, before the first meeting.

3 Be welcoming: This is the single most important factor in mid-week meetings. Within the team running each meeting, there should be one person whose specific task is greeting people and making them feel at home. Give everyone a badge so that the newcomers can learn names and build relationships. Also the whole team should make it their aim to speak to newcomers and welcome them. This example also rubs off on other church members who attend and so a culture of welcome is affirmed.

4 Be generous: Often mid-week events in the community are about making money, or covering costs, but the Christian faith is about God's generosity to us. So, if at all possible, do not charge for drinks, and give people home-baked cakes rather than just biscuits. This makes people feel special and loved, and they will want to come back. A donation box can be made available if people want to give.

5 Be Christian: Think about ways in which the good news about Jesus can be included in every meeting. This does not have to be done in a 'heavy' or forced way, but neither should it be relegated to the last five minutes or omitted for fear of embarrassment. Experience has shown that older people appreciate a 'thought for the day' style talk, and non-Christians are very happy for their children to sing toddler praise songs! The message is 'we enjoy our Christian faith, and you are welcome to join in'. Give regular opportunities for people to take their faith journey further through such things as Daytime Alpha, a bookstall and prayer ministry.

For reflection and discussion

1 What mid-week meetings do you already have in your church?
2 What does your church need in order to establish a mid-week outreach programme?
3 What personal resources do you have or need to build such a programme?
4 What opportunities are there for your church to break out into new markets with new products and services?

Great Idea 60

Face Up to It – It's a Business

JOHN NELSON

> If anyone does not know how to manage his own family
> how can he take care of God's church?
> 1 Timothy 3.5
>
> **Top Tip:** Church leaders need to recognize, accept, nurture and
> lead the management functions of their church.
>
> **Business Perspective:** Successful organizations understand the
> importance of learning from other organizations.

Scratch the surface and very quickly you will discover that ministry in today's church relies upon all the fundamentals of management. Most management titles and functions are taken directly from the commercial world and in some cases they are forced upon the church. You will find in every diocese the following titles which are by no means exhaustive:

- Systems manager
- Support assistant
- Director of property
- Property accountant manager
- Project development manager
- Commercial property asset manager
- Head of strategic development
- Strategic development support officer
- Director of personnel development

This list makes evident that the church does rest upon a foundation that relies upon specialist disaggregated managerial knowledge.

Notice the use of the words 'director' and 'manager', words often scorned and dismissed by some clergy in favour of the much more comfortable and less managerial terms.

Why? Because once such terms are accepted the natural consequence is to accept their function which is one of performance, measurement and accountability. All of which are directly connected to profit which is connected to customers and customer-oriented products.

A major barrier to thinking about the church in management terms is the word 'profit'. It is not helpful to think about profit in monetary terms but to reinterpret profit as the desired outcome for the church.

This is the key and essential difference between the church and other forms of secular commercial business. The church's aims are fundamentally different insofar as they are ultimately spiritual. However, the church still needs to be profitable and is profitable when it fulfils its purpose.

To fulfil its purpose in today's world it requires people with specialist managerial competence who can only work effectively in the context of sound leadership. Consequently those in church leadership positions need to recognize, accept, nurture and lead the management functions of their church.

The good news is that God has gifted human people with these skills.

God's business can only be achieved by a church which uses all the skills that God has provided. Leadership and management belong together just as much among the people of God as in the rest of the world.

For reflection and discussion

1 Discuss leadership and management in a church context.
2 What is the difference between leadership and management?
3 Why do we need leadership and management?
4 In what way is your church a business?

Great Idea 61

Incorporate the Green

DAVE BOOKLESS

> We know that the whole creation has been groaning
> as in the pains of childbirth right up to the present time
> Romans 8.22
>
> **Top Tip:** Respect and care for the planet.
>
> **Business Perspective:** Successful business organizations are
> customer led. They recognize that many customers have become
> concerned about green issues and by incorporating this business
> dynamic into their operations, products and services they
> encourage customers to emotionally attach themselves to the
> organization. Emotional attachment improves profitability.

A healthy church takes the whole Bible seriously. Caring for creation is essential to biblical mission, recognized today as one of the
'five marks of mission'. As churches today increasingly recover
what it means to care for creation in practical ways, they are also
discovering that it not only fulfils our responsibility to rule justly
and lovingly over the earth and its creatures, but it also:

1 Refreshes the faith of church members as they link the beauty
   of the earth and the changing of the seasons to their relationship with God
2 Attracts new people, both friends and family of church members who enjoy doing practical outdoor work, and those who
   have previously rejected Christianity as irrelevant to today's
   environmental crisis

3 Enables the church to be seen as 'good news' in its community, giving visible expression to the transforming power of the gospel.

The Bible begins with God's creative love for all he has made and he has given us the responsibility and privilege to protect and steward God's earth. It ends with God's plans for a renewed and restored heaven and earth, with Christ at the centre.

In-between, all the Bible's major themes have ecological implications. The fall leads to destructive relationships between human beings and the natural world, and yet the Psalms affirm creation's continued role in pointing to God's character and majesty. God's covenant with Israel is intimately connected to their stewardship of the land of Israel, and their continued failure has catastrophic environmental consequences.

Modern societies have often neglected the Bible's clear teaching about creation's potential to lead people to God, and about our human responsibility to protect and give answer to God for our stewardship of his world.

To create a profitable green product in your church you need to:

1 Preach and have Bible studies about creation care.
2 Start a 'green group' comprising key church members.
3 Audit your building, grounds and community to see what the environmental needs are.
4 Identify a practical project your church can initiate or support. Good examples include: turning church grounds into a nature study area; developing a community food-growing project; organizing a programme of nature walks followed by a short service of thanksgiving.
5 Renew the building through friendly insulation, solar power and other renewable sources.
6 Have a regular Sunday 'green' focus using harvest, world environment day, creation time, the changing seasons.

For reflection and discussion

1 What has having a green agenda to do with management and leadership in the church?
2 In your own church what lead can you take in showing that you care about the planet?
3 How can having a green agenda promote mission and ministry to your local community?
4 What form of green audit do you need for your church?

Great Idea 62

Keep Critical Statistics

A Case Study

PETER BRIERLEY

Mark was the new minister and everyone looked forward to his leadership. He was excited about all the possibilities too, believing this was where the Lord had sent him for the new stage of his journey. He knew he would have to review his performance at some stage, so he decided to keep a record of how things were going. What were the key facts he should record?

In a church situation the question is always, 'How many attend?' but total numbers need to be broken down by key parameters. So Mark decided that once a year, for every week in the month of October, he would keep a note of how many came to each service he held both during the week and on Sunday, and would count the numbers broken down by age: under 15, 25–29, 30–44, 45–59, and 75 plus. He chose age because, of all the factors in current church life, age of attenders is the most critical for formulating future policy. He made out a simple form and then completed it.

The key principles being followed were:

1 A decision to base future action partly on facts and not just on opinion.
2 An evaluation of how future policy would probably be decided and the information necessary to feed those decisions, in this case, age of worshippers.
3 Resolving when to collect the data, where to collect it, and

how, in this case, as his church was quite small, by personal observation; but he might just as easily have delegated the task to others.

4 Constructing a mechanism by which the relevant data could be recorded.

5 At some stage, an analysis of the results would be made and with it the decision to continue or amend the collection process, as well as considering changing policy or action in the light of those results. If collected data is not used, it might as well not be collected.

Engaging in the research process is important. It enables a church to inform itself with better information so that more suitable decisions may be taken. Such research does not always have to be quantitative; qualitative can be perfectly acceptable for making decisions. The following steps are offered as to the kind of research that is needed prior to starting out on a new venture.

Q Do you want to launch a new product?
A Evaluate your potential market audience.

Q Do you want to start a new service?
A Consider who might attend.

Q Are you starting a new ministry?
A Consider the needs of the people you will be approaching.

Q How do you address the huge question, 'Are you wanting to extend the kingdom of God?'?
A Ask the smaller question, 'Which groups of people could you most readily and naturally reach?' and, if necessary, ask some of those people what they would like you to offer.

Quality research depends on having a sufficient number of responses, although the size of sample will vary according to circumstance. However chosen, the number must also be representative of the group that is being considered. Asking a large number of people all with a similar experience or from the same background is usually not as helpful as going to a smaller but more diverse selection of individuals.

Whatever mode is used for collecting information, it is essential that it is well analysed. That often means not just saying '60 per cent said they liked the new leaflet' but rather indicating '40 per cent of men reading the leaflet approved of it but 75 per cent of women did not'.

That is, break down the basic data into appropriate segments such as gender, age or location, or, if relevant, denomination, churchmanship, size of church, age of minister, or environment such as city centre or council estate. Collecting similar data over time is especially important, trends can be seen which will enable you to forecast.

Facts are the fuel which the Spirit of God may use to direct, inspire and to challenge. They are always worth keeping.

For reflection and discussion

1 What was the business case for keeping critical statistics?
2 What do you think will be the future business benefits for engaging in market research for your church?

Great Idea 63

Know What Faith Is

BEN REES

What the Church is about can only be understood from within the Church, never outside it. To human reason, the doctrine of the Church is presumption or foolishness. No body of knowledge, and no statesman or government, can comprehend what the Church is, except through faith in Jesus Christ, the faith that he gives.

Great Idea 64

Know What's Important

A Case Study

PETER BRIERLEY

'Well, today I need to complete the last part of Sunday's sermon, choose the readings for the Sunday after that, visit Mrs Smith who is still in hospital, meet with the Luncheon Club ladies who feel they can't cope much longer with so many coming, order some more toner for my printer, and it's my turn to meet our seven-year-old at school.' Twelve hours later, Revd Brian Wagstaff reviewed his day. He had met his daughter from school, and had promised the Luncheon Club ladies he would try and find more volunteers, but there had been that long phone call in the morning about the next deanery meeting, and Jack the churchwarden had called to say the organist had had a very bad fall and could he go round and see her (which he did), and find a replacement for the Sunday service, but now it was too late to order the toner and he just felt too tired to complete the sermon. Mrs Smith got postponed. A typical day?

There is a huge difference between imagined priorities, what you hope to achieve, and real priorities, what you actually do. Too often circumstances, people genuinely needing help, or some seemingly very urgent task all crowd in to rob us of the hours needed to achieve what we had aimed to do. The issue is essentially the effective and flexible use of one's time. Ultimately the management of our time revolves around the management of oneself. If we haven't the self-discipline to do some things more than others then expect priorities to generally defeat us.

Real priorities ideally revolve around three broad areas:

- Putting things right
- Keeping things going
- Doing new things.

Putting things right is teamwork, so Brian was right to ensure he talked to the Luncheon Club ladies, but he now needs to prioritize finding the promised volunteers. This involves deciding how it should be done, as well as when it will be done and by whom.

Keeping things going is his daily work, so if he was freshest in the morning as many are then that should have been the time to complete the sermon. What then of the phone call? He should have not allowed that interruption. 'I'm sorry, John, I can't talk as I'm under pressure just now. Could I phone you tomorrow afternoon or could you send me an email about it?' He would then have had the satisfaction of having next Sunday's sermon completed instead of the nagging worry that he must do it tomorrow when tomorrow was already crowded.

Doing new things is leadership, and sorting out the readings for Sunday week, presumably a reasonably quick task, should have been part of his accomplishment. It would have helped whoever had to find readers to do their job more efficiently.

Ultimately, priorities revolve around the urgency we give to something and the importance we attach to that particular task. Both of these also revolve around the value we place on our actions. Brian rightly made meeting his daughter a vital task, so whatever he did that day, collecting her from school would be certain to feature.

Identifying our priorities through listing all our jobs and marking them A, B or C according to their importance today (the letter may change tomorrow) is a simple task, but overlooked. If we are to be successful it requires disciplined determination. Priorities may have to change during the day. For example, if someone calls wanting to know how to become a Christian, something should be postponed in favour of the enquirer. Cheerful flexibility must go hand in hand with dutiful prioritizing.

> **For reflection and discussion**
>
> 1 What was the business case for prioritizing your workload?
> 2 Evaluate the efficiency of your current workload priority system.

Great Idea 65

Learn How to Listen

KEVIN HUGGETT

I seek not those who affirm what I already believe and do, but those whose different approach and belief challenge me deeply, and teach me truly to listen and learn.

Great Idea 66

Learn to Live the Life of Love

TONY MCCAFFRY

> I have come that they might have life and have it to the full
> John 10.10
>
> **Top Tip:** The answer to all of these vexing questions is love.
>
> **Business Perspective:** Successful organizations create managers and leaders whose primary loyalty is to the organization, its values and its intent. However, such loyalty is not a constraint: it is the space which allows individuals to fulfil their potential while creating profit for the organization. Often this space creates conflict between the individual and the managerial realm. The art of leadership is in creatively managing this conflict. This can only occur if everybody in the organization recognizes that well-managed conflict is profitable. It rests primarily on trust and respect.

The word 'vocation' is one of the most important in the religious vocabulary. It is about discerning what God is 'calling' a person to be as well as to do.

A sceptical reader of my curriculum vitae might judge that the discernment process had been somewhat erratic. It is hard at times to respond to a God who enjoys drawing straight with crooked lines! It can be very hard to discern just what it is that God is calling us to be and do.

The Lord's Prayer asks for God's kingdom to come and God's will to be done on earth as it is in heaven. Many Christians confuse this 'kingdom' with a fixed geographical one. The simple addition of a verbal noun transforms 'kingdom of God' to 'the ruling of God' leaving plenty of room for 'the will' to be expressed and sought continuously.

This also provides improved grounds for seeing the working relationship to be one of altruism rather than egocentrism. Such relationship is indeed divine.

In seeking to do God's will consider these questions:

1 Which God is being served? Mine? Yours? Ours? A histori-cally conditioned fabrication? One fashioned in my own image and likeness? The definitive article or a love relationship in the course of development requiring careful daily attention?
2 Where is this God to be found?

God is to be found in the dynamic trinity of creation, redemption and sanctification. Every human being is a unique manifestation of the Godhead, an epiphany of the divine through their graced insights and relationships whether it is seen that way or not.

For anyone purporting to be a minister of such a God, conflict-ing loyalty tensions are not unusual. How many ministers face this dilemma: 'Do I do what I am told, or do I do what I see to be God's will, even though it rocks the boat and threatens my Church career?'

For reflection and discussion

1 Why should a loving response lead to conflict?
2 Where is the kingdom of God most present in your situation?
3 What is God's will for your church?
4 What is God's will for you?

Great Idea 67

Let My People Serve!

PETER BUNKER

Then I heard the Lord asking 'whom should I send as a messenger to my people? Who will go for us?' And I said 'Lord I'll go! Send me!'
Isaiah 6.8

Top Tip: The dissenting view can often unlock the truth.

Business Perspective: Successful organizations understand that profitability comes from passing as much of the operational costs as possible on to the customer. This entails getting the customer to be part of the production line of the organization. The more they are involved in producing the end product, the less cost the organization has to expend. This releases time and money for more profitable and strategic use.

Human beings need leadership and human society cannot operate without it. Because of the general situation today, authoritarian approaches are suspect, rightly so, and any would-be leader who assumes that he is entitled to exercise authority because of his traditional position will run into problems.

This is particularly difficult for clergy of all denominations. Even in the Free Churches, there is a strong assumption by some ordained ministers that they have some special right, almost an exclusive right, to leadership in many spheres of the churches' life. Where this combines with class assumptions of the privileged middle class, assumptions increasingly challenged in society, there can be quite painful experiences.

The resistance of the ecclesiastical structure to change and to challenge is such that a great many potential church leaders, not only among the laity but also among the best of the clergy, give up the struggle and get out.

On the whole, churches have not adjusted to a society in which it is taken for granted that there should be the right to question and to confront each other in honest disagreement, trying to find a greater truth through their disagreements. Until that sort of problem can be faced, any comments on how to produce more and better church leaders is really a waste of time. Let me share my own experience.

Whereas many of my friends were called to the ordained ministry or to the mission field, I was 'called' in just as true a sense, to be a layman in the church in England. I went to see the Revd Dr John Huxtable having been asked to undertake a major task for the Congregational Church in England and Wales. I told him my problem was with the Church itself at all levels. It often seemed to me irrelevant and sometimes got in the way of the mission of Christians in their service to his kingdom.

He smiled his sweetest smile and said, 'Yes, we know that. That is why we want you to do this job, despite your difficulties with the Church. Your gifts are valuable. If the Church is not able to welcome and use people with your kind of outlook, what hope have we for the future?'

The role of ordained ministry is crucial to the life of the church. But equally important is the role of those with different gifts and responsibilities, who are called to be lay people.

It doesn't stop there. We are also called to be ourselves and that means church ministry must accommodate and value those whose attitude and outlook of church is different to what might be considered mainstream or conventional thinking. All of us, with all that we are, are necessary to constitute the people of God.

For reflection and discussion

1 Am I enabling every member of my church to grow in active discipleship as co-workers with me in the mission and ministry of the church in this place?
2 Am I aware of the different gifts and skills of every member of this church community whether active or passive?
3 Am I actively engaged in the mission and ministry of this church in a way which propagates the gospel of Christ in my community?
4 What training or development do I need in order to enable me to serve the Lord actively in my local community?

Great Idea 68

Listen Twice Speak Once

JOHN SENTAMU

My mother used to say to me 'Sentamu, you have two eyes, two ears and one mouth. You use them in proportion: see, listen twice and speak once.' My top tip would be: Listen to God and see what he is doing; listen to others and see them as your brothers and sisters; and speak the truth in love.

Great Idea 69

Live in and of the Faith

CHRISTOPHER MAYFIELD

Encourage oneself and other people to live with both faith *in* Jesus and with the faith *of* Jesus. For he, despite uncertainties, suffering and the frailty of his best friends, devoted his whole life to working for the coming of God's kingdom here on earth.

Great Idea 70

Look Again and Check it

IAN THOMPSON

First impressions count: Christians are able to instinctively judge when something they see or come across is right or wrong. The same is true in respect of health and safety. When you see something for the first time or with fresh eyes and it looks wrong, then it is likely that it is wrong.

Great Idea 71

Maintain Your Spiritual Health

SUE HOWARD

> I pray that you may enjoy good health
> 3 John 2
>
> **Top Tip:** Spiritual health applies to you and to those around you.
>
> **Business Perspective:** Successful leaders and managers understand the relationship between physical and spiritual health and discipline themselves to ensure their well-being. They also understand their responsibility for the physical and spiritual well-being of the workforce.

There are obvious parallels between spiritual and physical health. Good health needs maintenance, so we are told to take in five or more portions of fruit and vegetables per day, drink plenty of water, take regular exercise and make time to rest and relax.

How fit are you physically? It's never too late to start to get in shape. Set yourself some physical challenges. The training will require a certain amount of commitment and discipline but the benefits are not just physical. You will feel better about life in general, more optimistic, less tired mentally and have more zest for living.

Spiritual training produces similar unexpected benefits. It is a holistic endeavour.

How fit are you spiritually? The tactics for getting physically fit are transferable to spiritual fitness. Train with others! Others can motivate you not only to keep at it, but to progress further than you might push yourself. The same can be said of church and prayer communities. We need each other to not only stay motivated, but to move ever closer to God.

There are various ways in which spiritual fitness can be prioritized. Many find it particularly helpful to identify a prayer partner. Pray together twice a month. Over a period of time this discipline will enable you to disclose more and more of your spiritual challenges to each other and, looking back, you will see that many of your prayers have produced spiritual fruit.

Encourage the activity of prayer partnering at your church using the following steps:

- Pray for guidance as to who you can pray with.
- Agree to meet based around times that you *can* do, not those you *can't*! (By that I mean set a timeframe that is realistic and which you can stick to.) Plan a period to test this spiritual practice, say for three months, and then gauge how helpful it is.
- Keep a journal of prayers (so you can review spiritual growth and how prayers have been answered).

For reflection and discussion

1 What is the relationship between physical and spiritual well-being?
2 How do you assess your own spiritual health?
3 What strategies can you put in place to encourage spiritual health and well-being in your church?
4 How spiritually healthy is your church?

Great Idea 72

Make the Most of Your Buildings

KEITH WILLIAMS

> Go up into the mountains and bring down timber and build the house, so that I may take pleasure in it and be honoured
> Haggai 1.8
>
> **Top Tip:** Leave no space left unused.
>
> **Business Perspective:** Successful business organizations understand fixed costs. As a consequence they maximize their infrastructure to increase profitability.

Who do the buildings of the Church really belong to? The buildings belong to God and not to us, and God is clear that they are for his pleasure and where he can be honoured. So we must make sure that we maintain them and make the most of them to fulfil his purposes. The book of Haggai is a reminder that we must get our priorities right and that the use of the buildings must reflect God's priorities not ours.

To understand God's priorities we need to listen to what he says to us through the Bible, the life of Jesus and the inspiration of the Holy Spirit. The message is loud and clear that the buildings are not a club house but for worship, doing his work and fellowship. The church is the people but the buildings are resources provided by God to build the body of Christ and bring him glory.

To make the most of our buildings we need to be doing God's work to the full, not just on Sundays but throughout the week. The buildings play an important part in supporting outreach and for service that demonstrates God's love in the communities in which we live – places for teaching and discipling to equip people and send them out; a physical beacon to draw people in; and places of hope and healing where the needs of individuals are met in a loving and safe environment.

All the rooms in the buildings can perform many different functions during the week – large halls can be used to hold large community events and run youth clubs or mother and toddler groups to make contacts; smaller teaching rooms can be used to build closer relationships through craft activities or special interest groups; kitchens and welcome areas can be used to host regular lunches for the elderly or the homeless.

Our buildings are also places of fellowship, not only around Sunday worship but also through works of service like maintenance and cleaning. Church DIY and cleaning days should not be considered as chores but rather as opportunities for God's people to work together to make his house a special place where he can be glorified, while sharing coffee and doughnuts together. We must also remember that everything we have belongs to God, so our homes should also be available as places of fellowship and hospitality, drawing people in and building them up as members of the church family.

Buildings will also be places of blessing for those who get the priorities right. From the day when the foundation of the Lord's temple was laid, God said, 'from this day on I will bless you' (Haggai 2.19). When we look at how we can make the most of our buildings we should do so with glorious expectations. '"In a little while I will once more shake the heavens and the earth, the sea and the dry land. I will shake all nations, and the desired of all nations will come, and I will fill this house with glory," says the Lord Almighty' (Haggai 2.6–7).

Great Idea 73

Make Use of Business Consultants

IAN OWERS

> Blessed is the one who finds wisdom and the
> one who gains understanding
> Proverbs 3.13

Top Tip: Sometimes a fresh perspective is useful to generate new ideas.

Business Perspective: Successful business organizations know when to and when not to employ business consultants. Most solutions lie within the organization. However, there are times when the organization experiences blockages in creative endeavours. It is at these times that using consultants can be cost effective, but such expenditure would not be committed until the organization had a very clear set of outputs. Consultancy for the successful organization is based on how to achieve, not what.

There is a lot of myth and nonsense surrounding consultancy, with both unrealistically high expectations and a considerable degree of cynicism.

There is also a wide variety of quality as well as variations of practice among consultants. Some will save time and expenditure by using standard processes and reporting frameworks that they regularly use. Others will prefer to develop the process according to your situation alone. While that can provide the greatest focus and be most effective in many situations, it is also more difficult for the consultant to assess in advance how much time and money it will take. In this case absolute clarity is essential about the parameters of budget, reporting and tasks required.

The following hints are designed to maximize the benefits and minimize the disappointments if you do decide to employ a consultant.

You need a particular expertise that you don't have within your organization (or, if you do, it's not appropriate to use it because of potential conflict of interest or other sensitivities). For example, architects or surveyors if you're planning or exploring a building project.

You may have the expertise, but you don't have the time. Very often leaders in faith groups and other voluntary organizations may well have the experience or expertise to undertake a piece of research, reporting or project development but other roles and issues within the organization are of greater priority. Rather than overstretching key people, it can be a good use of resources to buy in consultancy or other freelance support.

For vision building, strategic review or reflective Away Days it can often be invaluable to have a facilitator who is not engaged in the work or situation. Such a person can often help to bring an outside perspective or simply ask innocent questions that sometimes help participants to see their work or organization in a new light. At the very least, having an external facilitator will allow everyone to participate fully without having to chair, guide or take notes.

Be really clear about what you want out of the process, and write down what you want to achieve by involving them. Make sure that all the relevant people have been consulted and informed.

Check whether there are other external resources that could provide all or part of what you want. Very often there are church or voluntary sector infrastructure bodies that can provide some level of advice or support. At the very least, 'Google' the web for resources on choosing and briefing consultants.

If you've not used consultants before, speak to someone who has and learn from their experience.

Develop a really clear brief, including timescales, and decide how much you can afford.

Invite tenders and estimates from at least two potential consultants. Discuss how they envisage undertaking the work and how they have arrived at their estimate.

Ask for a CV or list of projects they have worked with, and for references or contacts who you can approach.

Do not use someone who has, or might have, any conflict of interest, including people within your organization or connected to them who might 'do it for free'. It's not just that it's more difficult to manage or address difficulties in such situations; very often organizations don't then do the essential work of being really clear about the brief and the project.

Do not expect too much for too little. One of the advantages of using consultants is that they can give focused, concentrated, high-quality attention to your project. That requires preparation, reflection and clear reporting. For example, facilitating a development day with preparation, planning, checking out and most importantly reporting back can sometimes take as much as three or four days of a consultant's time.

Do not always to go for the cheapest. First and foremost choose the consultant that most fits your brief. If budget constraints are severe, discuss this with the person you'd really like. Most consultants will have variable or discretionary rates, and most will be prepared to adjust the brief towards fitting your budget.

Sometimes organizations are not really sure what they want to do and hope that by bringing in an expert things will become clearer. This very often happens with building projects, when people bring in the architect at the earliest stage without being really clear as to what exactly they want out of a development or why they want it. Gatherings of consultants always quote this as one of the main reasons that building programmes go wrong and why people fall out with their architects.

177

For reflection and discussion

1 Which areas of your church's management and leadership would benefit from consultancy?
2 Which of the above suggestions have you found particularly helpful?
3 What are the biblical grounds for engaging consultants?
4 Which areas of your own life would benefit from consultancy?

Great Idea 74

Make Your Church a World Church

ANTON MÜLLER

> We were all baptized by one spirit into one body
> 1 Corinthians 12.13
>
> **Top Tip:** Look at what God is doing and join in!
>
> **Business Perspective:** Successful organizations harness the
> potential and possibilities of globalization to drive profitability.

Christians, and particularly Church of England Christians, may at
times feel despondent about church growth. All too often we may
hear news of how the Church is in decline. It can all too easily
seem very gloomy but the reality is very different.

While church attendance in the West and particularly the UK
is declining, that decline is partial. In parts of the UK the Church
of England is experiencing falling numbers. Churches are closing or ministers find themselves overwhelmed by the number of
churches over which they preside. But also it is a fact that some
churches are growing and some of those are Church of England
churches! Other denominations are experiencing amazing growth,
new small or cell groups are emerging all the time and this is
something to celebrate.

It is important to remember and celebrate that the Church is
a global organization. The Church is 'all God's people' all over
the world. A very tiny proportion of the Church in the world is
Anglican and a very tiny portion of the Anglican Communion
is represented by the Church of England. We get completely the

wrong idea of the Church of God worldwide if we view it only through our own local experience of it.

So does this mean that we can relax? Does this mean we can sit back and be content that all is well and there is nothing we need do?

By no means! The harvest is plentiful but the workers are few. We may represent only a tiny part of it but as the living body of Christ we must learn to live in the full knowledge of the whole. Thinking globally and acting locally may seem like a cliché but it is a very practical way of functioning as a World Church.

So how does a church become a World Church? It helps first to understand what the words mean.

A World Church is a world-aware church: it is curious about what God is doing worldwide; it is interested in, concerned for, excited with, encouraged by and caring about the lives of people who make up the church in the world.

A World Church reaches out into the world; it is involved with it through prayer, financial giving and sharing of resources. It also receives from the Church in the world through prayer, songs and liturgies, stories and people.

Here are a few very simple tips for bringing a world dimension to your church:

1 Support the mission agencies. This shouldn't be random but part of a co-ordinated strategy for mission that functions ecumenically and across the range of agencies. This is important as the agencies generally represent different parts of the world. Some churches have their own strong links with other churches or projects in the world but for most churches, the local branch of Churches Together could serve as the co-ordinating body for a locally based strategy. Those with their own direct links should still aim to be part of the wider locally based strategy and should exercise considerable care and prayerful discernment when going it alone to support individual churches or projects.

2 Involve the whole church by ensuring that different parts of church life and worship are informed by the life and worship of different church communities in the world. Engaging with

the Church in the world should not be sidelined as the concern of a few no matter how faithful the few may be. Your church can be touched by what God is doing all over the world. It is not just about singing songs from India or saying prayers from Africa, or reading out the occasional missionary letter. It is about identifying and entering into the real life experiences of Christians around the world. Anything less can come across as trite, patronizing, colonial and insulting!

World music, prayers and liturgies are not an end in themselves to spice up the occasional service, they are a window into the lives and stories of God's people who share with us an experience of a relationship with the one God who calls us into one family worldwide.

3 Encourage curiosity to know about the people we aspire to call our brothers and sisters in the world. As brothers and sisters we are co-heirs not custodians of all that God gives to us through Jesus. Our involvement with other church communities should be about sharing good practice in the kind of leadership that promotes healthy spiritual growth.

4 Be prepared to be challenged and to take part. The challenge may be recognizing that you have more to receive than to give, more to learn than to teach, more to listen than to speak.

Archbishop Desmond Tutu once described mission in the world as 'seeing what God is doing and joining in'.

For reflection and discussion

1 How does the wider church impact upon the life of your church?

2 What kind of involvement do you have with mission agencies?

3 What leadership and management practices from other churches in the world could help you in your own church situation?

4 How will you enable your church to be a World Church?

Great Idea 76

Manage Your Meetings

PETER BATES

> Everyone should be quick to listen and slow to speak
> James 1.19
>
> **Top Tip:** Ensure equality of influence by all members.
>
> **Business Perspective:** Successful organizations understand role and function and ensure that each role is undertaken by competent members of the organization. This is particularly important in meetings as they tend not to be productive unless properly led. The function of a meeting is to solve problems, generate news and to improve profitability.

Do you perform well or badly at meetings, and do you know why? 'Perform' applies because, as with a stage role, your contribution to a meeting is most effective if your performance is good. So how do you know if you perform well?

To become more effective you need to review and analyse your performance, perhaps with the assistance of an independent observer, perhaps by taking a recording of part of the meeting and being prepared to discuss the content as a group, with each of you being prepared to listen to others' comments on your performance, and to learn from them.

All members of a meeting have a role to play, but the major and, importantly, separate roles are chairmanship and input. These two roles are distinct and for those parts of a church meeting where the vicar is providing the main input it is recommended that someone else should take the chair.

In practice most of us involved in the community have to chair meetings frequently and we need to spend time in preparation and in monitoring our performance and effectiveness.

Drawing up the agenda is the first part of preparation, as agenda content and order are vital for a meeting to be effective. It can be useful to note on the agenda the nature of each item, for example, report, discussion, for decision, etc. Items needing careful consideration and decision should appear early when people are fresh, rather than later on when everyone wants to go home.

Time preparation is important so that the meeting does not run on, with members becoming weary. Try going through the agenda beforehand, assigning an estimated time interval to each item. Of course you will not keep to the estimate, but at least you will have a plan, and you can make adjustments as you go along and so avoid taking things in a rush at the end.

An ideal aim to keep in mind is to ensure equality of influence by all members, whether voluble or not. One of the most important chairmanship roles is to try to ensure that all members have an equal influence, and that the quieter ones are not dominated by the more vociferous or eloquent speakers. This is especially important where members are present in a voluntary capacity and membership has a pastoral dimension.

Everyone should be quite clear on the decisions taken and their own part in any resulting action. This can be achieved by including in the minutes an 'Action' column, containing the initials of anyone who has agreed to or been designated to take on all or part of that action.

Lastly, AOB. Any Other Business (or perhaps 'Urgent' Business) has a role to play, but do not let it dominate the meeting. Generally decisions should not be taken under AOB unless absolutely necessary. Use the slot to give notice of items which need full consideration and decision at subsequent meetings.

Being responsible for a successful meeting can be very satisfying. Hopefully by following these guidelines and taking time to prepare, train and learn from experience, your own performance can help to make your meetings both effective and enjoyable.

Great Idea 77

Manage Yourself

Worksheet

MICHAEL LOFTHOUSE AND
ANTON MÜLLER

The purpose of this worksheet is to encourage you to personally reflect.

Complete the following worksheet. Do not spend a long time considering each statement. We recommend you answer quickly, instinctively. Please photocopy the following page to create your worksheet.

The acid test would be to give this worksheet to somebody you trust will answer truthfully about you and then compare your answers to theirs. Are you brave enough to do this?

If you have answered No to any of the statements we suggest you list them in priority order, the first being the one that has the most impact on your management of your church. Then with someone you trust work through the questions in order of priority over a period of time and obtain feedback that will help you.

I am able to recognize my emotions and the effect they have on others	Yes	No
I am able to control my emotions and not let them dominate my management decision making	Yes	No
I am always confident in management situations	Yes	No
My perceptions in management situations always aid my decision making	Yes	No
I always exercise self-control	Yes	No
My management team considers me to be trustworthy and conscientious in matters related to the management of our church	Yes	No
I am always ready to be adaptable	Yes	No
I am goal oriented in managing my church	Yes	No
I am persistent and not deterred by adversity in the management of my church	Yes	No
I am receptive to others' needs and emotions in management situations	Yes	No
I am willing to use the emotions of others in sustaining and growing my church	Yes	No
I am willing to challenge behaviours that hinder the good management of my church	Yes	No
I am a team player	Yes	No
I am an effective management communicator	Yes	No
I am an effective leader in the management of my church	Yes	No
I am committed to sustaining and growing my church through effective management	Yes	No

Score

1–4   Yes answers – who is managing your church?

4–8   Yes answers – demonstrating a management foundation to your church

9–12 Yes answers – nearly there, I want to work with you

13+   Yes answers – you should have contributed to this book!

Great Idea 78

Mind Your Own Business!

JOHN ADAIR

All leaders worthy of the name grow their businesses. The first question you have to ask yourself is what business are we in? The business of the Church is the business of Jesus, 'my Father's business', namely the coming of the kingdom of God. When did your congregation last ask themselves the question, 'What business are we in?'

Great Idea 79

Move on into New Ways of Being and Doing

LEN SIMMONS

> Open our eyes that we might see the wonders of your word
> Psalm 119.18
>
> **Top Tip:** The art of seeing in a new way has to be applied to the very systems of governance and organization of the Church.
>
> **Business Perspective:** Successful business organizations understand and implement the lessons from their history. They are not trapped by what has occurred in the past but convert what they know into productive management information which informs and grows the organization. They encourage their workforce to accept and learn from their decisions and actions by engendering a no-blame culture.

The very fact that you are reading this book suggests that you will be looking for ideas to grow a healthy church. Hopefully you are not looking for a quick fix, for if so the rest of this section is not for you.

Jesus invites all of us to 'repent and believe the good news', to make a clean start and to move on into new ways of being and doing. 'Repent' is the change word, but even the meaning of that word has been changed. The Greek word chosen by the early bilingual church for the Aramaic word spoken by Jesus is *metanoia*, which means 'change of mind or repentance'. The change called for was deep within human nature, truly revolutionary – to have the mind and spirit of Jesus.

Metanoia is the essential manifestation of 'regeneration' that sets us straight in our relationship to God and so radically alters our perspective that we begin to see the world through God's eyes, not our own. Only then can we grow a healthy church.

Individually we practise reflection, self-examination, confession and repentance but do we ever do this to the corporate body of the church?

The application of *metanoia* to the actual organization of the whole Church at every level is essential in order to achieve the 'regime' change that Jesus proclaimed. The kingdom of God is the regime: the regime in which the motive power is the power of goodness itself, effective in the goodness of all human relationships. This would lead to the fulfilment of 'the hopes and fears of all the years': the putting right of all that is wrong; transformation; reformation; rebirth from above; renewed creation!

In its most radical form regime change might well be what Jesus described as mending old garments with patches of new cloth. The old is not strong enough to hold the new and the tear is made worse. Or storing new wine in old wineskins; the skin cannot withstand the pressure of the desired fermentation gases and bursts.

For Jesus the desired regime was of love. Entry was free and unconditional, the gracious gift of the effective love lived and taught by Jesus and finally poured out by his God and Father in raising him from the death of crucifixion. This is the new cloth, the new wine. But what of the garments? What of the wineskins? What of the human organization required to contain this new life? What are the instruments required for this regime change? Discerning these things is the task facing you and your church if you are to become healthy, whole and fit for service.

For reflection and discussion

1 How would you encourage open and free management discussions within your church?
2 How do you reward those members of your church who are prepared to tell you uncomfortable things?
3 What do you understand by a no-blame culture church?
4 What do you need to do to prepare yourself for a no-blame culture church?

Great Idea 80

Move Your Vision from Me to We

PATRICK GOH

You are the body of Christ and each one of you is a part of it
1 Corinthians 12.27

Top Tip: Visioning processes take account of the whole body.

Business Perspective: Successful organizations understand that a vision statement is not a policy document.

Apart from Jesus' manifesto in Luke 4 have you ever been truly inspired by a vision statement that you've seen in church? Your answer probably depends on how much you were involved in helping to craft the statement and how much of your passion you see reflected in it.

Rather than inspiring people to action, attempts to write vision statements tend to leave people vaguely amused but cold. This is because it is almost always the expression of the vision of one person or, at best, the leadership team. This is out of step with the biblical principle in Joel 2.28 where God says that he will pour out his Spirit on all people: 'Your sons and daughters will prophecy, your old men will dream, your young men will see visions.' If we take this to be true, surely visioning processes should take account of the whole body.

Vision statements embody assumptions about the nature of leadership, which can be examined and placed within its underlying theoretical contexts. In this sense, they serve as windows on the worldview of the people who crafted them.

Even organization researchers have begun to acknowledge that 'mission or vision statements are centrally produced and managed information systems', which are obvious attempts by management to 'impose general rules about the organization'. This research showed that lower grade staff regarded the authors of the statements as elite groups imposing their values on everyone else.

Rather than feeling inspired, they feel marginalized because the statements feel like a closing down of conversations by a 'monologic discourse'. This also applies to church members.

In the community we call 'Church', what would happen if vision statements avoided imposing a unitary grand narrative and used approaches that genuinely reflect and celebrate diversity? The sheer numbers of people that make up church makes it polyphonic or multi-voiced. While in theory we say that we value diversity, in practice most evangelical churches have tended to take the line that 'we can only work together if we agree on everything first'. While it is true that the grand narrative has its place, the question is how to express it in the local context. It needs to be in conversation with everyone who serves in that context, not just the leader/s.

If we do have to have vision statements, we would do better by designing a process where everyone can speak with their own unique voice and experience, making their own agendas explicit. In such a process, the role of leaders is to facilitate a visioning process that connects different voices with common ground for action; and creates a common sense of how to go on. This is done by helping people to genuinely listen to each other; to appreciate diversity; and to use the multiplicity of views as a resource and strength to meet this challenge.

For reflection and discussion

1 Is your church governed by a grand narrative or by a vision generated by your church?
2 Through what narrative process has your vision statement been generated?
3 Is your current vision statement a policy document or strategy for present and future ministry?
4 What is your role in generating new thinking, vision and direction in your church?

Great Idea 81

Offer Quality Worship

MICHAEL LOFTHOUSE

Worship the Lord in the splendour of his holiness
1 Chronicles 16.29

Top Tip: Customers provide the revenue to generate the wealth of the Church, both physically and spiritually, and are its reason for existence.

Business Perspective: Successful business organizations understand their customers – both present and potential – are able to segment their customers and offer products and services that meet their needs and aspirations and fulfil the organization's purpose.

A customer-driven church:

Is an attractive church

It is responsive to customer needs and is innovative and responsive in combating the threats posed by the competition, not least the attractive products offered by the secular world.

Is a listening church

It strives to provide real value to each customer at an individual level both physically and spiritually.

195

Is an added-value church

It provides a safe, welcoming and appropriate infrastructure, both physically and spiritually, that enhances all of its products and services.

Is an accessible church

It offers quality products and services.

Is a relevant and consistent church

A successful church needs to attract and keep customers. It needs to turn customers into converts and congregations. It needs therefore to offer quality products and services. Customers are attracted by quality, informed as they are by their secular experiences. Customers are the arbiters of quality.

Ministry must be surrounded and supported by quality products and services.

But what is quality? It is a shifting and subjective concept but it can be shaped. Church leaders are required to engage in an ongoing hegemonic discourse with its customers to establish and maintain quality thresholds. Delivery of the product or service must match or preferably exceed these quality thresholds. Remember the customer is also part of the products and services offered by the church. Customer participation in the design and delivery assist in establishing and maintaining quality. But quality does not necessarily mean a flawless product or service. Nor does it mean the most expensive. Quality products and services deliver as expected.

The design of a quality product or service is an interconnected linear management process (see Figure 6).

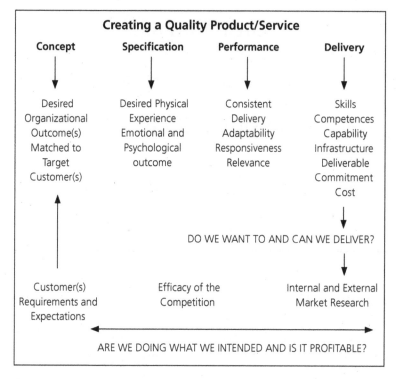

Figure 6

Being able to create specifications for each of the elements outlined above assists in creating and sustaining a quality product.

For reflection and discussion

1 Performance – how well are you doing?
2 Features – are your customers happy?
3 Reliability – are you consistent?
4 Conformance – do you meet (exceed) the pre-established standards?
5 Sustainability – can you maintain quality products and services?

Great Idea 82

Plan Ahead and in Detail

A Case Study

PETER BRIERLEY

The newly appointed minister had made a good initial impression in her first few months. Angela planned the next month or so well ahead and told all those involved what was needed. She discussed with the Church Council plans for the coming year and knew what they thought about her suggestions. Then she said, 'I'm going away for a week to plan the next five years.' She wanted to begin the process of recasting the church's vision, and knew the initial draft which would then be shared with the Council would require undisturbed concentration. After five years what decisions would the Council have wished they had made? What did the church, under God's guiding hand, want to become? What image would the church have in their neighbourhood? How would they answer the question, 'Oh, you go to St John's? That's the church which had a vision for ...'?

There are broadly two ways of generating vision: you can plan ahead from where you currently are or you can imagine the future and plan backwards to meet where you are. Both methods work, and different leaders will not always achieve similar results. Angela was one of those who worked with the first method, so she tried to answer the following questions.

What was the purpose of the church for which she was responsible? She decided it was 'To reach out in evangelism and service'. Others might choose a different phrase starting with 'To', and expect that the Church Council would agree.

What was the work that the church overall was currently doing? This is what many would describe as mission. She decided it was 'Making Jesus known', but again others would use different phrases, each starting with a present tense participle ending in '-ing'.

Then came the crunch question. In the light of these answers what did she believe the Lord was calling her church to become? What was the vision? Should it be expressed numerically or qualitatively. Angela thought the challenge of growth was important, so she would suggest for discussion with her Council, 'To become a congregation of 180 from our present 120 in 5 years' time.'

The fourth question is then, 'What steps do you have to take over the next five years to make that vision become reality?', and so Angela listed eight steps which she felt the church could take in the next 12 months, and a further six for the 12 months after that, again for discussion with the Council.

Such statements can be made for any church. Note that Angela, effectively the CEO for her church as in an organization, felt she should initiate the discussion on future vision, but her ideas would have partly come from her prior discussions with others, as well of course as its final ratification both by the Church Council acting as her Trustees and then the whole church.

For reflection and discussion

1 What was the business case for creating the vision and strategy?
2 What do you think will be the future business benefits of creating an agreed vision and strategy?

Great Idea 83

Plan Good Public Relations Worksheet

MICHAEL LOFTHOUSE AND
ANTON MÜLLER

The purpose of this worksheet is to provide you with a performance checklist to enable you to evaluate the efficacy of your public relations interventions.

I have a sound working knowledge of the methods and the technology involved in generating and distributing effective stories about my church	Yes	No
I know how to construct a story. I know it is about ensuring I answer each of the questions posed by Who? What? When? Where? Why? How?	Yes	No
I know a good story is about: People An angle My church Truth – but remembering the power of emotion Selling, selling and selling Keeping the story short and digestible Selecting the appropriate media for the chosen audience	Yes	No
I am confident that I can generate regular good news stories about my church	Yes	No
I understand how to play the percentages, taking the instances of bad news in my stride	Yes	No
I continuously educate and train myself in public relations practices	Yes	No
I understand that every encounter is a public relations opportunity	Yes	No
Public relations is a fixed agenda item at my church management meetings	Yes	No
I understand that perception is more important than truth	Yes	No
I understand the role public relations plays in sustaining and growing my church	Yes	No

Congratulations if you have answered Yes to more than six statements. You understand the importance of public relations in the life of your church

If you have answered No to any of the above statements take the next step and answer the question why? This will generate a list of issues that you can use to generate discussion at your next management meeting.

Great Idea 84

Prepare Your Congregational Vision

PHILIP PLYMING

> You will be my witnesses in Jerusalem and in all Judea and
> Samaria and to the ends of the earth
> Acts 1.8
>
> **Top Tip:** Vision is a process not an event.
>
> **Business Perspective:** Successful organizations understand that
> it is common in the commercial world to articulate a vision. Put
> simply a well-constructed and articulated vision informs those
> inside and outside the organization who the organization is, what
> it does and why it does it. Churches also need a well-constructed
> and articulated vision.

While it is essential to have a corporate vision each strategic business unit (the parish) also needs a vision.

Corporately it is about discerning where God wants to lead us and as such is an essential component of a healthy local church. Without vision a church tends towards maintenance, introspection and decline. With it a church is equipped for mission, outreach and growth.

At local level vision is best discerned not only by the church leader, or by committee, but by the whole church, who will then own it. It is best to think of this as a vision process that is led by both vicar and community. It is essential that this process takes account of the corporate vision.

It is essential that you let the church know you are leading a vision process to discern the future for the church. Uncertainty leads to inefficiency. Ask them to pray with you and work with you.

It is essential that you ground the process in Scripture, mindful of the corporate strategy to be witnesses and disciples.

In a commercial venture the decision-making process would be led by a raft of management information. As a church you can do this by following these simple steps:

- Gather those are who are able and willing to help you
- Produce a prayer booklet that has Bible passages and tips for prayer in it
- Encourage church members to share their thoughts with you at any stage
- Outline the timeline for the vision process
- Keep all participants informed and grounded

Remember, a vision cannot be achieved unless it is feasible, acceptable and sustainable.

You also have to be grounded. Take yourself away and pray for the future of the church, noting down Bible passages that speak to you and what you notice about church and community life. Share what you have discovered in practical terms with a group of people you trust who may well form the team you will need to manage the vision initiative. Follow these steps to building your vision team:

- Your team should be no larger than six people and with a cross-section of age and gender, should include people who know the church well, know God well, and can think creatively about the future. It is not just for the great and the good!
- This group should work with you to analyse data about where the church is now, look at the Bible's vision for the local church and pray about where God might be calling you. Over a few meetings a number of common strands are likely to emerge.
- Repeat the above process until the vision is complete. Again, use data, the Bible and prayer. A day away can be a good time to do this.

- Have an update meeting with the whole church and community to share what has been sensed so far. Emphasize this is part of the vision process, not the end of it.
- Give every person a piece of paper on which they can write their response: what excites them about this imagined future? What makes them nervous?
- Reflect on and distil with the team the responses. Finalize your vision and add objectives.
- Finally, have a church meeting at which you share the vision of your church, address any concerns and talk about the future. Celebrate the fact that you believe God has guided the church, and look forward to the future.

Vision is a process, not an event.

For reflection and discussion

1 Who is willing and able to assist the church in formulating a vision?

2 Are you open to new and challenging ways of thinking about the future of your church?

3 Are your management systems capable of capturing and distilling the ideas generated by your team?

4 Does the capacity exist to convert the consultation process into a meaningful vision statement?

Great Idea 85

Process and Structure

Worksheet

MICHAEL LOFTHOUSE AND ANTON MÜLLER

The purpose of this worksheet is to encourage you to reflect, receive feedback and competently lead your church into fruitful discussion that is management focused on growing your church. Please photocopy the worksheet and write in the spaces.

It is the structure and resultant processes of your church that forms the foundation of all you do and how you do it.

Consequently it should be very carefully defined, particularly in respect of processes, cost, size and complexity. It is here that your professional knowledge and experience will overlap and complement your management knowledge. Of course if you do not possess the relevant management knowledge then it makes good business sense to acquire it. Seeking added value and competitive advantage through an effective church structure is the constant.

Exercise

List all of your church activities; these can be considered as the products you offer. Make sure the list is exhaustive and disaggregated. Against each activity detail the processes and structures that are required to support and sustain delivery. State who is responsible for the delivery of each activity. It is useful to encourage that person to provide the information. A useful approach is to start with the delivery to the customer and work backwards listing all processes and structures that are required. This can lead to an effective method of costing each activity.

List any gaps between current structures and processes and effective delivery and what needs to be changed. You can cost the required changes.

An important additional question that is generated by this exercise is which of those activities in the way it operates and its outcomes is the closest to the strategic intent, purpose, of your church and why. You may even stop doing something. You may even change your structure and processes.

Great Idea 86

Reach Out

ROD JACQUES

A healthy church is always there for that time when a person becomes isolated and feels they are in a strange land. A church always reaches out.

Great Idea 87

Reflect, Receive and Report

Worksheet

MICHAEL LOFTHOUSE AND
ANTON MÜLLER

The purpose of this worksheet is to encourage you to reflect, receive feedback and competently lead your church into fruitful discussion that is management focused on growing your church. Please photocopy the following page and write in the spaces.

Self

Answer the question: How is the church a business? Don't be trapped by previous experience or understanding of church. Try to step outside your current role and examine your church dispassionately and with a clear intention for it to succeed and grow.

Justify your conclusion below in no more than 50 words.

Others

Share the above with someone you trust who will give you an honest opinion rather than what you want to hear. Remember that positive and negative comments will assist your understanding of the task ahead.

Disaggregate

Utilize your reflection and the feedback you have received to introduce the topic at your next management meeting. Ensure that you record all contributions. This may be a difficult and painful process for some.

Great Idea 88

Samaritans – A Structure for Support

A Case Study

BILL DOUGLAS

Samaritans operate with a very particular emphasis on support.

Here, support is taken to mean the kind of emotional and psychological help a person may need to withstand tough situations. Many have experienced the anguish of being stuck in a crisis, burdened unbearably, or facing the no-win scenario.

This support is built into the structures at all levels, and guided by a disciplined approach to ensure our best possible service to callers.

Samaritans is a national charity with 17,000 trained volunteers in 201 branches across the UK and Ireland. Each branch is also a charity responsible for how they organize their own business matters. Periodically a branch director and a chair of trustees is appointed from among the volunteers.

All branches work according to nationally agreed principles and practices, and get help from paid staff headed by a chief executive in General Office. All branches are involved nationally on policy and practice issues and in periodically electing a national Chair. The governing Trustee Board, two-thirds of whom are Samaritans, is advised on policy by the Council of Samaritans, on which all branches are represented.

So, Samaritans is a volunteer-led movement, supported by paid staff.

Samaritans aim to provide confidential emotional support to anyone in distress, despairing or suicidal. This support is available 24/7 to callers, whether contacting by phone, face-to-face, email or text.

Volunteers are trained to listen carefully, engage, and respond to help callers with their feelings. Engaging with people in traumatic situations can be stressful.

In recognition of this, support is built-in at branch level for volunteers responding to callers. While branches vary in how they organize their work, there is an essential requirement for a minimum of two volunteers on duty who can support each other, and a shift leader to support, mainly through debriefing. A duty director is always available for consultation.

To support front-line activity, teams of volunteers tackle recruitment, selection, training, outreach, prison work, and speaking, awareness and fundraising events. With all of these activities it is mandatory movement-wide that there are always at least two volunteers involved. Support is also provided through annual training, available in every branch for every volunteer.

Built into regional and national levels are channels of support for volunteers. This is essential if the organization is to keep improving its care for callers.

The organizational structure of Samaritans reflects a caring ethos throughout. This humanitarian approach in a secular organization also radiates a central message of the Gospels which is to show love for one another by supporting one another, as well as having a structure of support.

It is not uncommon for some clergy who through too narrow a view of confidentiality or through an unwillingness to burden others, feel unable to speak of their experiences with anyone.

Whatever the pattern of organization, but especially those involved in aspects of care in the community, whether secular or religious, it is vital that a structure of support exists and is available to the workforce. Such a structure is vital to safeguard the carer and the client, the volunteer and the caller, the parish priest and the parishioner.

For reflection and discussion

1 What was the business case for Samaritans to implement a structure of care and support for its volunteers?
2 Evaluate the effectiveness of your systems and structure for care and support in your church.

Great Idea 89

See the World as Christ sees the World

HEATHER HOPFI

A priest friend of mine once told me that we should try to see the world through the eyes of Christ looking down from the cross with compassion and love for suffering humanity. I have always found this perspective inspiring and a lesson in how to see other people.

Great Idea 90

Serve by Leading – Lead by Serving

ELIZABETH WELCH

> If I, your Lord and Teacher, have washed your feet,
> you also ought to wash one another's feet
> John 13.14

Top Tip: Know, understand and appreciate the value of the menial and the majestic.

Business Perspective: Successful organizations understand that their leaders and managers must know and understand their staff as well as their customers. Leaders and managers must understand the work across the whole organization and value each person's contribution as vital and significant. This does not negate their primary responsibility which is to the organization. However, difficult decisions can be made within a framework of compassion and understanding.

The last supper passage in John 13 is a paradigm of servant leadership and possibly the most quoted scriptural passage on this theme. However, it's also a passage which is easy to quote out of context, without taking the time to dig below the surface of Jesus' encounter with Peter. It is often used as a mandate to work harder and give more of oneself to others, to the point of exhaustion.

Entering more deeply into the encounter between Jesus and Peter opens up a wider range of perspectives on the nature of service and leadership. Peter, in his usual impetuous fashion, either rejects the idea of being washed, or wants to be washed completely. At first sight, his rejection of being served sounds like a worthy reflection of his own desire to serve. It's only when he comes under pressure of strong words from Jesus that he has a change of heart. Then he swings in the opposite direction, wanting to be washed all over. With each swing of the pendulum, he has placed himself at the centre of attention rather than focusing on his calling as a disciple of Jesus.

Jesus combines the integrity of purpose needed in a leader, with the ability to carry his purpose through, while demonstrating that his leadership is nonetheless about service. He walks the fine line between wholehearted commitment to his followers and his own dedicated sense of where his life is going. Servant leadership is about discerning the needs of others and responding, while not getting so sucked into those needs that the original sense of God's calling disappears.

In his ministry, Jesus balances the time he spends with the disciples and with the crowds, and the time he spends on his own in prayer. He had a limited time with the disciples and was faced by many needs in the crowd. In the midst of this, his attentiveness to his own need for nourishment and renewal strengthened the leadership he offered to those around him.

Serving by leading and leading by serving means holding together these qualities that Jesus embodied. It means balancing the willingness to meet the needs of other people who present themselves day by day, with attentiveness to the leader's inner needs and ultimate sense of calling. Too great an attentiveness to the needs of others can lead to a loss of sight of the bigger picture and exhaustion setting in. Too little attention to the needs of others can bring the onset of arrogance and a style of leadership that is removed from that of the servant. It can be like walking a tightrope.

To develop a servant style of leadership you could try some of the following:

- Take time each week to locate and reflect on a biblical example of servant leadership
- Ask others to let you know what they think of your leadership and management style
- Keep a 'spiritual balance sheet' between leading and serving.

For reflection and discussion

1 What is your understanding of servant leadership?
2 What do you require to develop a servant leadership style?
3 What currently best describes the leadership in your church?
4 What criteria will you use to assess if your servant leadership style is successful?

Great Idea 91

Strive for Healthy Growth and Unity

VINCE NICHOLS

Pray often, personally and as a community. Be welcoming. Be patient. Keep the focus on the Lord who alone gives us growth and unity, as St Paul says to the church in Corinth, 'I planted, Apollo watered, but God gave the growth.'

Great Idea 92

Take 'An Hour Out'

JOHN PRITCHARD

> Until all of us come to the unity of the faith and of the knowledge of the Son of God, to maturity, to the measure of the full stature of Christ
> Ephesians 4.13
>
> **Top Tip:** Create space for people to talk about their faith journey in a confidential and safe environment.
>
> **Business perspective:** Successful organizations understand that clinical supervision and mentoring are commonplace. These things have become an important part of helping people to deal with difficult situations in the workplace alongside helping people grow in their professional competencies. Successful organizations set time aside for this process.

A healthy church is one where God is clearly and unequivocally at the centre. Yet we are often reserved when it comes to talking about God, finding it easier to talk about churchy activities rather than the glorious reality at the heart of it all.

In order to break through this barrier consider the idea of 'an hour out' whereby church leaders offer to anyone in their congregation an hour, within a set period, to talk about their spiritual journey. Many churchgoers wish they could talk confidentially about what they do and don't believe, their joys and struggles with prayer, what they'd like to understand about the Bible but never dared ask, how to apply their Sunday faith to their Monday lives, and so on.

An hour out offers people an hour's undivided attention from someone they trust, be it their priest or minister or lay leader. An hour out is an opportunity to say whatever they like. For ministers, it allows them to do what they always want to do but rarely get the chance, to talk with people about their deepest feeling concerning their faith.

By focusing on this opportunity once a year, both congregations and ministers are given permission to do what they might not otherwise be able to find a way of doing. It builds up confidence, honesty and faith, and above all it keeps the spiritual journey alive and moving.

To implement an hour out programme:

1 Produce guidelines for the minister and the lay person. For example for the minister the advice includes: don't rush, encourage and never put people down, listen to what is really being said, ask open questions such as, 'Where did your faith journey start?' 'What would you like to understand better?' 'What do you do when you pray?'

   For the lay person the guidelines include: decide beforehand what you'd like to discuss, only say what you want to say, be bold and don't be left thinking 'if only I'd said ...'

   • Talk about the main thing, that is, you and God
   • Say what you value about faith and where you get frustrated
   • Ask if there's something you could read
   • Write down afterwards what you've learned

2 To prepare for the programme, the leaders need to announce that they are offering this hour to anyone who wants to talk about their spiritual journey. Invite people to phone or email to fix one of the times you have reserved. Think about and gather the resources that you will find most helpful in conducting the session.

3 You will need to allow time to overcome people's reserve, but when it becomes known as a normal, faith-developing experience, it helps a church to grow in honesty, openness and trust. It also enables people to talk with each other and with those

outside the church about matters of faith. God is then spoken about and not kept as an inner secret with doubts attached.

For reflection and discussion

1 What benefit could 'an hour out' have for yourself and other members of the church?
2 What are your current arrangements for giving space for church members to talk openly about their faith?
3 What emotional and organizational strategies do you need to properly implement 'an hour out'?
4 What would you do if the church member identified **you** as the biggest obstacle to their spiritual well-being?

Great Idea 93

Teach the Whole Counsel of God

RICHARD HIGGINSON

There is no substitute for teaching the 'whole counsel of God' –
opening up the Bible to show its relevance to the whole of life.
This requires a combination of intellectual rigour and imaginative
application: the judicious juxtaposition of word and image; and a
sensitive understanding of God's purposes revealed through salvation history. What a privilege it is to share in such teaching.

Great Idea 94

The Children Shall Lead
if we Let Them

A Case Study

SOPHIA SCHUTTS

St John's, Newton Reigny, is a very small parish of 190 house-holds. Part of the benefice of Penrith, a town of 40,000 with two Anglican churches, St John's parish consists of two small villages. There are about seven working farms, a pub and several holiday-lets. About half the residents are retired. Several residents are employed by the county police HQ in Penrith. Some residents commute to Carlisle or further afield. The children of the parish go to several nearby primary schools or to one of the two second-ary schools in Penrith.

The PCC was concerned that those teenagers who had been con-firmed were not having much or any connection with the church. A parent of two teenagers suggested that, since the front church-yard gates were rotting and needed replacing, we ask the young people to come up with suggestions and designs. The PCC agreed and specified that the new gates should be wrought iron because the wooden ones had not lasted long. It was also specified that the gates should not be too solid or seem to exclude the public.

At a meeting of young people the idea was eagerly taken up. Several designs were submitted and were displayed in the church for comment. The favourite was by the great-granddaughter of the donor of the original gates. The group of six or seven young people then came up with a composite design based on the favourite, which showed the outline of a church in the middle. The PCC voted to submit it to a nearby metalwork company to see if it was practical. The company manager said he could produce it and sent his blueprint. The PCC then voted to apply to the diocese for a faculty.

This process had taken about two years because PCC meetings are infrequent and teenagers are busy, and the parish had no priest with special responsibility for the parish. Another several months elapsed before the diocesan committee replied with a negative and no explanation. We replied giving more explanation and with photos of the back and side gates which are metal.

We then requested a site visit from the diocesan committee, but the archdeacon, who was the chairman of the committee, came alone. He was supportive of our proposal but the diocesan committee wanted a gate similar to the wooden one being replaced. A compromise was agreed between the archdeacon and the PCC secretary that the gate could be metal, but that the design should be traditional, based on the design of the existing side gate.

At this point I moved away from the area and handed the business over to the PCC and the parents of the teenagers, who were, by this time, thoroughly disillusioned. As far as I know the matter has been dropped, but I am not sure.

The moral of the story, if there is one: There can be a conflict of interest between those who seek to guard the status quo and artistic integrity and those who wish to encourage ownership of the church by the young and their parents.

Two of the young people involved in the project continued to be involved for a while in the life of the church.

For reflection and discussion

1 What was the business case for allowing the young people's gate design?
2 What do you think will be the future business benefits for the church following the decision not to allow the young people's design?

Great Idea 95

Time Your Work and
Plan for Neglect

PETER BATES

Use the present opportunity to the full
Ephesians 5.16

Top Tip: Leave undone some of those things you should have done and there will be health in you!

Business Perspective: Successful organizations understand that their primary asset is people and expend energy to ensure their psychological and physical well-being. Healthy people are productive people.

Time is the most important and valuable resource given us by God, and it is available to everyone in exactly equal amounts. Analysis and examination of our use of time is therefore vital – we have a duty to think how best we can and should use the 24/7 hours that God has given us.

What measures of time usage can be adopted by the minister, the volunteer or each of us as church members and leaders? Freedom to use time as we wish carries with it responsibility to manage that time usage effectively. We need to understand when we are wasting time, even with the best of enthusiasm and intentions.

Studies of clergy time usage have shown the average priest in parish ministry 'working' for 61 hours a week, made up of 16 hours' public and private worship; 9 hours' reading, study and instruction; 8½ hours' visiting and counselling; 10 hours' administration; 11 hours' meetings (formal and social); and 6½ hours' travel.

A fundamental question raised by these figures is what is work for a minister, and the same question applies to voluntary workers and lay people when acting in church leadership roles. The definition of 'work' can be especially difficult in these circumstances. So much of the time expended could also be defined as 'social', and questions arise about which of our activities are properly 'work' and further, how taxing the activity is in work terms.

Because we experience conflicts of time in the duties and activities that we undertake, it is necessary sometimes to adopt a policy of planned neglect, which arises in the Rule of Life from the Companions of Brother Lawrence:

In order to live a fully rounded life, life as God intends it to be, we must include things other than our work. Almost inevitably this means leaving some things undone. For us, planned neglect will mean deliberately choosing which things we will leave undone or postpone, so that instead of being oppressed by a clutter of unfinished jobs, we think out our priorities under God and then accept without guilt or resentment the fact that much we had thought we ought to do we must leave. We shall often be tempted into guilty feelings when we do take time off, but we should then remind ourselves that such guilt is a sin against the generosity of the Spirit, and also extremely infectious.

The Rule emphasizes the importance of all our activities, including volunteering, time off, family and relaxation, all of which must be taken into account when we decide which we should neglect.

One method for measuring your own use of time is at the end of each day to jot down in your diary a rough estimate of the percentage of your time spent on each of your six or seven major activities. At the end of each week or month add up your recorded figures and you will have an ongoing record of where your time has gone, and hopefully some idea of whether it has been used to best effect.

For reflection and discussion

1 How do you prioritize and define your work?
2 How do you manage your time off?
3 How do you ensure the psychological and physical well-being of others?
4 How do you measure your own psychological and physical well-being?

Great Idea 96

Vary Your Worship Style

DAVID JAMES

In our own language we hear them speaking about
God's deeds of power
Acts 2.11

Top Tip: When Sunday worship is interesting, attractive,
enjoyable and vital, the 'passing through' becomes the
'occasional', the 'occasional' becomes the 'regular' and the
'regular' becomes the 'committed and involved'.

Business Perspective: Successful organizations understand that
packaging is as important as the product.

When we meet together for worship we give expression to what
we claim to believe about God and about ourselves as the people
of God. We dare to hope that we might have an encounter with
God which will make a difference to our lives as individuals and
to our life together. With something like 70 per cent of the adult
population claiming to be people of faith and over 40 per cent
believing they have had a spiritual experience, there are far more
people who cross the threshold of our churches who have that
same hope, however tentative.

The reasons for the massive discrepancy between 'faith' and
church attendance are many and complex but some of the responsibility lies with those of us who plan and lead our worship. If we
wish to reach out to those who have felt the wind of the Spirit
but do not know from whence it comes and we can focus on only

one thing, it must surely be our worship. To quote the manual for 'Leading Your Church into Growth': 'When Sunday worship is interesting, attractive, enjoyable and vital, the "passing through" becomes the "occasional", the "occasional" becomes the "regular" and the "regular" becomes the "committed and involved".'

Imagine as a Christian being a guest at Friday prayers in a mosque. The experience there is usually one of great courtesy and warmth. And yet, for Christians and non-Muslims everything going on in the mosque may seem alien: the totally bare room except for carpet and a reading desk; the language of the prayers and the closely choreographed kneeling belong to a completely different culture. Many people today have almost the same experience when they enter a church. Christian worship and even places of worship are likewise culturally alien to the uninitiated. One minister has gone so far as to say that, 'People are afraid of the church building and afraid of our liturgy.'

From day one the Christian church has been culturally, socially and indeed nationally diverse. Over the centuries uniformity of worship has been used to give a sense of commonality or even as a form of control.

But diversity doesn't seem to be a problem to God, and whenever the church becomes introverted, protective of itself and authoritarian, the subversive generosity of the gospel manages to break out somewhere else, if necessary in a new church or a new denomination.

If we are prepared to shrug off the straitjacket of uniformity we can begin to offer worship which might be appropriate to people outside or on the edge of the church but not beyond the reach of the outstretched arms of Christ. Here are some simple suggestions:

1 Have a varying pattern of main Sunday morning services to cater for a wide range of people.
2 Offer extra services at a time best suited to the people you are seeking to embrace. Sometimes these services grow to have more worshippers than the 'main' Sunday service! The extra service could be a very traditional BCP evensong reaching a

particular segment of the community who find this style of worship uplifting.

3   Don't be constrained by Sundays. A weekday at a particular time may be far more practical for some families where Sunday has become busy with sports and clubs.

4   Think about introducing a 'cafe church'. In a 'cafe church' service people, young and old, sit around tables in a parish room or school hall. They begin the service with food and drink and chat. Sharing stories in these small groups often becomes an important part of the worship. Before starting a cafe church a certain amount of market research will need to be done to work out how, when, what and which segments of the community are most likely to benefit.

5   Don't reinvent the wheel. See what approaches other churches are using in other areas, even if they are not the same denomination as you.

For reflection and discussion

1   What different services could your church offer to your local community?

2   What training and resources will you need to manage additional services?

3   What would be the benefits of such an approach to your church and to your community?

4   What will be the success criteria for such a venture?

Great Idea 97

What are You Selling?

Worksheet

MICHAEL LOFTHOUSE AND
ANTON MÜLLER

The purpose of this worksheet is to provide you with a strategic list of questions that can be used to generate meaningful management discussion and decision making. Please photocopy the following page and write in the spaces.

Critical to the global success of commercialism is the support from the customer. Individuals are converted into customers by its responsiveness and predictability, and thereby promote the whole approach. For managers four dimensions dictate its success: efficiency, calculability, predictability and control. Participative control is exercised over the customers, while those who work in the organization are managerially directed and therefore controlled.

Commercialization and the Church

Fact   Your church is not the centre of most parishioners' lives and it isn't necessarily their most important activity.

Q   What can you learn from a commercial model of operation to alter your market position?

Fact   Parishioners want their church to operate like their supermarkets and fast-food restaurants as it is what they are used to.

Q   What can you learn from a commercial model of operation that would increase your number of customers?

Fact   A congregation is a collection of individual customers who demand individual service. They want to feel valued and an integral part of their church.

Q   What can you learn from a commercial model of operation that would generate and sustain individual service?

Fact   All present and future customers want of their church are simple procedures, good service, quality and low costs.

Q   What can you learn from a commercial model of operation that would deliver these essential elements of success?

Reflection 1: How does such a commercial approach to church management make you feel?

Reflection 2: Despite your initial reaction to these questions what have you learned that could be of use to you in managing your ministry?

Great Idea 98

Work Out Where You are Going

PETER BATES

> 'O Lord, God of my master,' he prayed. 'Give me success
> and show kindness to my master, Abraham.
> Help me to accomplish the purpose of my journey'
> Genesis 24.12
>
> **Top Tip:** Don't be vague.
>
> **Business Perspective:** Successful organizations understand that
> an efficient production line is driven by a set of clear objectives
> which includes what to do, when to do it and quantifies the
> desired output. This is often termed the operations manual.

When did you set out on a journey without knowing where you
were going – probably only at birth? For every journey that we
undertake during our lifetime, we need to define the destination
before we start.

That is the principle behind the discipline of Management by
Objectives, which had its heyday in the 1960s and could be trans-
lated as Ministry by Objectives. In practice, it is applied common
sense and provides an excellent framework for congregations,
synods and deaneries to examine what they want to do and where
they want to go over the next few years.

In the Synodical Government Measure of 1969 the functions
of a deanery synod are laid down and include this statement: 'to
promote in the deanery the whole mission of the Church, evangelistic, social and ecumenical'. That statement provides a good

agenda for deanery synods, and for congregations and church councils of all denominations, when considering their role in relation to mission in their church, parish or area.

It is the basis from which each can define the purpose of its mission activity and then formulate some aims or long-term objectives for achievement within three to five years, and some goals or short-term objectives for achievement in the coming six to twelve months. Short-term objectives are needed as well as long, because we all need to be able to recognize what we have achieved – looking three to five years in advance is too far ahead to grasp on its own. The three to five year aims provide the framework within which can be set the six to twelve month goals.

Congregations, synods, parishes and deaneries should be careful not to define too many objectives, both long- and short-term, and those adopted should be both realistic and challenging. Realistic in that they must be achievable, not pie-in-the-sky, and challenging in that real effort is needed if their achievement is to provide any satisfaction, both individually and collectively.

The three activity areas listed, evangelistic, social and ecumenical, provide a useful starter for all groups to examine their mission objectives and there follow some statements of purpose for each of these activities, which you and your congregation may like to use to begin your thinking.

Evangelistic to invite and attract nominal Christians and those untouched by Christianity to share in the Christian faith and life

Social to enable the local community to identify and meet its real needs

Ecumenical to promote and demonstrate the unity of the church in prayer and action.

For reflection and discussion

1 What does your operations manual contain?
2 Do all of your objectives have stated quantifiable outputs?
3 Does your operations manual set out the procedure for accomplishing your objectives?
4 What is your role and function in the operational management of your church?

Great Idea 99

Work to Build the House of Prayer for All Nations

JOE ALDRED

> And there before me was a great multitude from every nation, people, tribe and language
> Revelation 7.9
>
> **Top Tip:** Variety is the spice of life.
>
> **Business Perspective:** Successful business organizations understand the power of organizational culture both to improve and diminish profitability in a multicultural and global marketplace. Diversity within the workforce creates positive thinking and contributions.

People everywhere behave according to the well-known saying: 'Birds of a feather flock together'. This is true of tribes, clans, nations, cultures, vocations, faiths, denominations, and hosts of other bases of human interaction. The charge of Jesus to the Church to take the gospel to all nations has been variously interpreted as a charter for both monocultural and multicultural approaches to mission. And since the 1950s Britain has experienced the phenomenon of the 'Black Church' which for some represents a divisive development in an already divided society.

I am not troubled by the advent of the Black Church. I have grown up in one and that has not made me narrow in my view of the world or my perception about how society at large and the Christian Church in particular should look and behave. Indeed the often cited biblical imperative that in Christ we are neither Jew nor Greek, male nor female is open to interpretation and does not encourage too strict a literal meaning since I, writing this, am Christian and male!

As we scan the British scene we see churches that are made up of majorities and minorities of various types, the most obvious in a highly racialized society being skin colour. Black-majority and Black-led churches are ever present in urban areas, but so are White-majority and White-led ones; and a little below the radar we find Asian-majority and Asian-led churches, plus others.

Without desiring to artificially change what is, I have for some years now wished to see more churches of mixed ethnicities, led by someone from an ethnic minority background. The ones that exist tend to be White-led. I believe such a church would add even more variety to an already culturally rich tapestry of church belonging in Britain. How would one set about building such a congregation?

First, I have as my inspiration Revelation 7 where an enraptured John is in heaven and sees an innumerable multitude gathered around the throne of God in worship. They were from every tribe, nation and language. So we see that in this eyewitness account of heaven people are distinguishable by the very attributes that we are so often keen to suppress or undervalue in the name of Christian unity.

Actualizing this heavenly ideal of unity in diversity in worship, we would have a leadership team of three pairs or groups: one of Black African or Caribbean heritage, one of Asian or Chinese heritage, and one of White European heritage. As an object lesson the senior leader would be either Black or Asian. All three groups must be theologically trained to at least degree level. The senior pastor should be trained to masters or even doctoral level. Within the team there will be expertise in administration, mission, culture and politics. This means attention will be paid to all the members of the team and the training and gifts they bring.

Ethnicity will not determine ministry and so every effort will be made to ensure that ministry is non-discriminatory unless where mono-ethnicity is imperative. I believe that a deliberate bringing together of a talented, qualified and experienced multicultural leadership team would lead to a healthy and growing multicultural congregation. The initial timeframe to test this idea would be five years.

For reflection and discussion

1 What is the ethnic constituency of your church?
2 How does your church understand the idea of a house of prayer for all nations?
3 How open is your church to learning about the practices of Black- and Asian-led churches?
4 What can you do to increase awareness of what God is doing in the worldwide Church?

Great Idea 100

Work with the Workers

DAVID CLARK

> Live so that your daily life may win the respect of outsiders
> 1 Thessalonians 4.12
>
> **Top Tip:** Encourage and value the ministry of every church member.
>
> **Business Perspective:** Successful business organizations understand the marketing power of ensuring that their workforce are advocates for the organization both inside and outside the organizational environment. Successful managers value their workforce within the workplace and encourage them to sell the organization when outside the organization. A valued member of the organization will sell the organization to others.

What Christians do in and through their daily work is a vital aspect of the mission of the church. However, so often we neither know much about the work in which our fellow Christians are involved, nor ensure that they, and us, are supported in their ministry in daily life by the whole Christian community. One way to tackle this failure is through a 'St (your church's name)'s at Work' booklet. It should be made available to every church member. Here's why and how it's done.

The purpose is:

1   To enable the members of a local church to become more aware of the paid and voluntary work in which its members are involved during the week.

2 To celebrate the gifts that God has given them in order to be able to work for the coming of his kingdom.

3 To encourage all concerned to share experiences and insights about how the gospel might be shared in the different working contexts of each member.

4 To support one another in their working lives, not least through prayer and pastoral care.

The best size for this sort of booklet is A5.

The booklet should list the occupations of the paid or voluntary work in which church members are involved during the week. It may not be appropriate to give the names of the people involved as this information could be misused. It is also important to find ways of including and valuing those who do not work in the conventional sense of the paid or voluntary sector. Those who are homebound can also be encouraged to be valued workers for the Lord.

Include an introduction that sets out the purpose of the booklet for sharing work interests, praying for those at work and other kinds of support. It is important to include two or three prayers which people can use to help them in their daily work.

It is important that you prepare the whole congregation.

Ensure that the purpose of the booklet is understood and its production agreed by the church as a whole.

Print out postcard size cards on which members can write their paid or voluntary occupation(s). Give the opportunity for members to include their name if they wish, but assure them that this will not be included in the booklet and that the information they give will not be used for any other purpose.

Make clear that the information provided will be made public in booklet form (declaring the use to which information will be put is necessary to comply with the Data Protection Act).

Hand out the cards personally, over two or three Sundays, and ask people to put them, when completed, in a box provided for that purpose. If people are away, they should be mailed a card with a covering letter and reply envelope.

This kind of booklet can be of value to any church. It is amazing, even in small churches, how little some members know of the work that others do during the week.

Choose a person to head up the project who is a capable organizer and able to collate the responses into a draft booklet.

Ensure that the booklet is attractively produced. With IT resources this can usually be done inexpensively.

Make clear that the booklet will not include church offices or responsibilities.

If possible, link the launch of the booklet with a 'faith at work' service and/or display.

Ensure there is a reference to the booklet on the church website.

Revise the booklet as needed, but at least bi-annually.

For reflection and discussion

1 In what ways does your church support its members in the workplace?
2 What three things could your church do better to support its working members?
3 In what ways can your church link up with local businesses and places of work around it?
4 How can you help your church members develop their ministry of mission and evangelism in their workplace?

Great Idea 101

Worship, Lead and Manage

JOHN NELSON, MICHAEL LOFTHOUSE
AND ANTON MÜLLER

> If anyone speaks, they should do it as one speaking the
> very words of God. If anyone serves they should do it with
> the strength God provides so that in all things God may be
> praised through Jesus Christ
> 1 Peter 4.11
>
> **Top Tip:** Standing still is not an option.
>
> **Business Perspective:** Successful business organizations know
> that in order to be profitable and healthy the business must rest
> upon a foundation of effective leadership and sound management.

Ministry, leadership and management are components of the modern Church and they are inextricably linked. Proficiency in equal measure in each is essential. If deficiency in any of the components exist a profitable church is that much harder to achieve.

That is not to say that deficient churches cannot exist, they do. Often replicating, as they do, what has gone before, creating and sustaining an environment of steady and progressive decline. They are also a financial and spiritual drain on those around them.

Even if you are part of a successful, profitable, church this just means you have the critical managerial and structural mass from which to diversify, expand and grow. Standing still is no longer an option. Where you are succeeding, the competition is waiting for you to take your eye off the leadership and managerial

241

ball. Where you are failing, the competition has already filled the spiritual vacuum.

If you are part of a failing or managerially troubled church it is your duty and responsibility to lead your community forward in order to fulfil God's purpose.

The prescription for improving your leadership and management health is within your grasp. It consists of a large dose of commitment to the principles of leadership and management with additional injections of personal bravery and a realization that it is all right and quite likely that you will stumble and fall along the way. Indeed, if you are committed to improving your church, your leadership and management condition will almost certainly get worse before it gets better.

What's the big idea?

It is fundamental to Christian belief that we are created not only in the image of God but that God has breathed his life into us. We live as human beings whose souls hunger and thirst for God. Our spirits need to be fed and nurtured by God. It is surely one of the principal functions of a church that it provides the opportunity for the community around it to be spiritually fed and watered.

God calls the church to be a conduit of his grace, a channel for his peace and a fountain of his living water.

Too often churches are none of these things. Too often people find that the church, instead of symbolizing the feast of the heavenly banquet, is arid and dry, serving up the spiritual equivalent of gruel.

Churches and their leaders must wake up to the fact that there are many ways in which people can meet the spiritual hunger and thirst within them. In the marketplace of humanity the competition is endless and easily available.

We have in our grasp the bread of life and the wine of the kingdom but so often we present it as stale and lukewarm. No wonder people turn to the more enticing fast food outlets of contemporary spirituality only to find themselves hungry again in no time at all.

So, what's the big idea?

242

Well, appropriately, it's three ideas in one and it is very Trinitarian. The idea for every church is simply this: Worship, lead and manage.

1 Worship (God the Father): Does the worship offered by your church lift the soul and the spirit to God. Is it about God or is it about human traditions, culture and rituals?
2 Lead (God the Son): Is your church leading to and led by Jesus? Is Jesus Lord over the church or is your church under the power of others? It could be the PCC; it could be any number of individuals who exercise power over the leadership of the church. Every church has the equivalent of those who in some sense pay for their seats and expect to sit in them.
3 Manage (God the Holy Spirit): Does the Holy Spirit have full reign in your church? The Holy Spirit is the dynamic power of God which brings order out of chaos. A well-managed church will not be a chaotic church. A properly managed church will have a sense of order and purpose. There will be unity within a celebration of diversity.

In the pages of this book you will encounter a wealth of expertise, but also a wealth of experience, often unexpected, that you can use to help your church to grow successfully into a healthy and profitable church.

For reflection and discussion

1 Spend time exploring the questions raised in these three areas of worship, leading and managing.
2 On the basis of what emerges from this exploration, what do you need to do now?

About the Contributors

Sandra Ackroyd is a member of Vine URC in Ilford (Great Idea 27 Create a Holiday Club)

John Adair is a world authority on leadership. His many publications include *The Leadership of Jesus* as well as contributions to previous MODEM publications (Great Idea 2 Ask the Lord his Business; Great Ideas 78 Mind Your Own Business!)

Joe Aldred is a bishop in the Church of God of Prophecy. He is the secretary for minority ethnic affairs at Churches Together in England (Great Idea 99 Work to Build the House of Prayer for All Nations)

Roy Baker is a retired parish vicar, Merseyside (Great Idea 31 Develop the Talents of Others)

Peter Bates is a former professional management scientist in the electricity supply industry; founder member of CORAT and MODEM (Great Idea 34 Do the Things that Matter; Great Idea 76 Manage Your Meetings; Great Idea 95 Time Your Work and Plan for Neglect; Great Idea 98 Work Out Where You are Going)

Alan Billings is a parish priest and Radio 4 Broadcaster (Great Idea 37 Don't Throw out the Baby with the Baptism Water)

David Blunkett is an MP and former Cabinet minister (Great Idea 16 Be the Centre of Community not a Satellite)

Dave Bookless is the director of Theology for Churches and Sustainable Communities (Great Idea 61 Incorporate the Green)

Mike Breen is an innovating pioneer in creating missional communities throughout Europe and the USA (Great Idea 14 Be in the Business of Making Disciples)

Peter Brierley is the former director of Christian Research (Great Idea 62 Keep Critical Statistics; Great Idea 64 Know What's Important; Great Idea 82 Plan Ahead and in Detail)

Peter Bunker is a United Reformed Church lay leader in Sussex, and MODEM's legal adviser (Great Idea 67 Let My People Serve!)

Roger Bush is Dean of Truro and formerly Archdeacon of Cornwall (Great Idea 30 Develop and Grow Together)

David Clark is a Methodist minister and former presbyter, now member of its Diaconal Order, advocate of lay ministry and discipleship in the community and work situation (Great Idea 100 Work with the Workers)

Charles Clayton is the director of Oxford Leaders Ltd, and former CEO of World Vision UK (Great Idea 29 Delight in Leading Well)

Len Collinson is a business entrepreneur and consultant. He is Deputy Lieutenant for Merseyside (Great Idea 51 Explore the Skills You Need)

Peter Colwell is director of programmes, CTBI (Great Idea 43 Embrace the Social Media)

David Cornick is general secretary, Churches Together in England (CTE) (Great Idea 55 God has Provided – now Manage it)

Richard Dannatt is former head of the British Army and member of the House of Lords (Great Idea 28 Delegate with Confidence)

Paul Davies is vicar of St Mary's, Sunbury-on-Thames (Great Idea 26 Create a Community Arts Project)

John Devine is chancellor, Liverpool Hope University (Great Idea 4 Avoid Judging other People)

Bill Douglas is a Samaritans volunteer (Great Idea 88 Samaritans – a Structure for Support)

Philip Down is the archdeacon of Ashford, Kent (Great Idea 8 Be About Your Father's Business Part 2)

Jolyon Edwardes is a social entrepreneur, founder and MD of Good Connection (Great Idea 49 Expand the Community)

Bernard Foley is a former Liverpool University lecturer and writer on economics (Great Idea 35 Don't be Suspicious of Economics)

Richard Fox is a coach, facilitator and mentor in church leadership. He is director of a management and parish consultancy group and a member of MODEM's leadership committee. Richard is author of *Creating a Purposeful Life* (Great Idea 44 Enable Effective Partnering)

Darrell Gardiner is lay reader of Holy Trinity Church, Formby (Great Idea 48 Establish a Lay-led Church Plant)

Patrick Goh is head of global human relations, Tear Fund, and former head of human resources for the Church Mission Society (Great Idea 5 Be a Listening Church; Great Idea 23 Change the Way we Make Decisions; Great Idea 80 Move Your Vision from Me to We)

Charles Gordon-Lennox is Duke of Richmond. He has served as a Church commissioner, member of General Synod and on committees of the World Council of Churches. He was chair of Christian Organization Research Advisory Trust, the forerunner of MODEM (Great Idea 17 Be the Church of God)

Malcolm Grundy is former archdeacon of Craven, York diocese, first director of the Foundation for Church Leadership and former chair of MODEM (Great Idea 15 Believe that You too can Change the Church; Great Idea 19 Be Personally Effective)

Margaret Halsey is director of the Leeds Church Institute (Great Idea 39 Dream in Metaphors and Stories for Organizational Change)

Tim Harle is visiting fellow at Bristol University Business School, lay canon at Bristol Cathedral and vice-chair of MODEM (Great Idea 41 Embrace Change)

Greg Haslam is senior pastor of Westminster Chapel, London and member of the Fellowship of Independent Churches (Great Idea 45 Engage in Radical Surgery)

Richard Higginson is lecturer in Christian ethics and director of Faith in Business, Ridley Hall, Cambridge University (Great Idea 93 Teach the Whole Counsel of God)

Heather Hopfi is professor of management, Essex University (Great Idea 89 See the World as Christ sees the World)

Sue Howard is a Christian spirituality workplace consultant and former member of MODEM's national leadership committee (Great Idea 71 Maintain Your Spiritual Health)

Kevin Huggett is chaplain, senior tutor and guitarist at Furness College, Lancaster University. He was formerly assistant secretary, Africa region with CMS (Great Idea 65 Learn How to Listen)

Rod Jacques is a former prison governor (Great Idea 86 Reach Out)

Michael Jagessar is national moderator of the URC (Great Idea 27 Create a Holiday Club)

David James is former bishop of Bradford and chair of trustees of St John's College, Nottingham (Great Idea 96 Vary Your Worship Style)

Keith Lamdin is principal of Sarum College, Salisbury (Great Idea 10 Be Discontented!)

Michael Lofthouse is director of LM Consultancy, formerly deputy director of Canterbury Christchurch University Business School and member of MODEM's national leadership committee (Great Idea 7 Be About Your Father's Business Part 1; Great Idea 9 Be an Agent for Change; Great Idea 33 Do it for Them not for Yourself; Great Idea 50 Expect the Unexpected; Great Idea 58 Have an Ethical Propaganda; Great Idea 77 Manage Yourself; Great Idea 81 Offer Quality Worship; Great Idea 83 Plan Good Public Relations; Great Idea 85 Process and Structure; Great Idea 87 Reflect, Receive and Report; Great Idea 97 What are You Selling?; Great Idea 101 Worship, Lead and Manage)

Hugh Martyn is senior officer for Kent County Council, former senior police officer and lecturer in management for the National Leadership Academy for Policing, Bramhill (Great Idea 52 Fill Your Leadership Space)

John Kingsley Martin is with CMS and was editor of the Church of England Newspaper (Great Idea 32 Distil Some Passion Stew!)

Commissioner Elizabeth Matear is territorial leader of the Salvation Army in the UK and Ireland (Great Idea 21 Bring God into Everyday Life)

Tony McCaffry is a retired educator, but still active in adult religious learning within his RC tradition, between traditions and between religions (Great Idea 66 Learn to Live the Life of Love)

Christopher Mayfield is former Bishop of Manchester and MODEM chair (Great Idea 69 Live in and of the Faith)

Anton Müller is an Anglican priest. He has leadership and management experience gained through both parish and community-based ministries, is a tutor with Lancaster and Carlisle Training Partnership and former member of MODEM's national leadership committee (Great Idea 6 Be Able to say Sorry; Great Idea 33 Do it for Them not for Yourself; Great Idea 36 Don't Recruit – Evangelize!; Great Idea 4 Make Your Church a World Church; Great Idea 77 Manage Yourself; Great Idea 83 Plan Good Public Relations; Great Idea 85 Process and Structure; Great Idea 87 Reflect, Receive and Report; Great Idea 97 What are You Selling?; Great Idea 101 Worship, Lead and Manage)

Sue Müller is a nurse with 30 years' experience as a practice, community and district nurse and latterly at Hospice at Home and the Eden Valley Hospice (Great Idea 40 Embrace those on the Final Journey)

John Nelson is national secretary of MODEM and editor of MODEM's four previous books on management, leadership and ministry (Great Idea 13 Be 'In-house' and 'Out-house'! Great Idea 20 Be Witnesses in the Workplace; Great Idea 60 Face Up to It – It's a Business; Great Idea 101 Worship, Lead and Manage)

James Newcome is Bishop of Carlisle. He was minister of Bar Hill Ecumenical Church for 12 years. He has leadership experience as an Anglican rural dean, and theological college tutor. He was director of ministry with Chester diocese before becoming bishop of Penrith (Great Idea 1 Agree a Vision)

Vince Nichols is the Roman Catholic archbishop of Westminster (Great Idea 91 Strive for Healthy Growth and Unity)

Ian Owers is a Sheffield-based independent third sector consultant with special knowledge of faith-related community involvement (Great Idea 73 Make Use of Business Consultants)

Colin Patterson is part of Bridge Builders, Mennonite Centre (Great Idea 46 Engage Openly with Disagreement)

Rebecca Paveley is a freelance journalist (Great Idea 22 Care for the Co-habiting)

Ben Pennington is director of PR firm Polaris based on Merseyside (Great Idea 54 Get Social with the Media)

Philip Plyming is vicar of Holy Trinity, Claygate, Surrey (Great Idea 59 Hold Mid-week Meetings; Great Idea 84 Prepare Your Congregational Vision)

John Pritchard is Bishop of Oxford (Great Idea 92 Take 'An Hour Out')

Ben Rees is a minister in the Presbyterian Church of Wales and professor of ecclesiastical history at the North Western University, South Africa (Great Idea 56 Have a Biblical Vision; Great Idea 63 Know What Faith Is)

Joe Riley is art critic and political columnist for the *Liverpool Echo* and *Daily Post* (Great Idea 12 Be Inclusive, not Divisive)

Kath Rogers was priest in charge at Holy Trinity, Formby (Great Idea 53 Form a Messy Church)

Roberta Rominger is general secretary of the United Reformed Church (Great Idea 47 Engage in the Power of Adverstising)

Peter Rudge is a church management pioneer (Great Idea 18 Be Mindful of Management

Sophia Schutts is a retired teacher and PCC secretary (Great Idea 94 The Children Shall Lead – if we Let Them)

John Sentamu is archbishop of York (Great Idea 68 Listen Twice Speak Once)

Len Simmons is a management consultant, former director and manager in newspaper publishing, and chairman of MODEM East Midlands group (Great Idea 79 Move on into New Ways of Being and Doing)

Phil Simpson is CMS Asia director. He has been with CMS for 25 years. He is a former missionary with experience working on drug rehabilitation projects, based in Karachi and Peshawar. He trained in social work and worked as a probation officer (Great Idea 38 Dream Dreams)

David Taylor is a doctor at Liverpool School of Tropical Medicine and a locally based NSM (Great Idea 11 Be Friendly with Science and Medicine)

Ivor Telfer is a lieutenant colonel with the Salvation Army (Great Idea 24 Come for Tea, Come for Tea my People)

Ian Thompson is a health and safety international consultant (Great Idea 70 Look Again and Check it)

Ian Tomlinson is a multi-benefice rector in Winchester diocese (Great Idea 57 Have a Metric for Rural Church Management)

Michael Volland is director of mission and tutor in pioneering at Cranmer Hall, Durham (Great Idea 75 Make Yourself into an Ordained Entrepreneur)

Elizabeth Welch is chair of MODEM and former national moderator, United Reformed Church (Great Idea 90 Serve by Leading – Lead by Serving)

Keith Williams is a financial management consultant and former member of the national leadership committee of MODEM (Great Idea 25 Count the Cost; Great Idea 72 Make the Most of Your Buildings)

Terry Wynne is a politician and former MEP (Great Idea 3 Aspire to be Great)

Richard Young is a venture capitalist, NSM and clergy mentor (Great Idea 42 Embrace Failure)

About MODEM

MODEM exists to enable churches to explore and engage with managerial and organizational issues. Its primary task is to lead and enable authentic dialogue between exponents of religious and secular leadership and management leading to more effective church (and secular) management.

Formed in 1993 as a national network of clergy and laity, it became a nationally registered charity. It quickly established itself as the voice of leadership, management and ministry leading to its current position as a hub for leadership, management and ministry. It is an associate member of Churches Together in Britain and Ireland.

It replaced the former Christian Organizations Research and Advisory Trust (CORAT). In 1991 CORAT decided to call a consultation meeting of all interested parties to review its work over the previous 20 or so years and to determine whether or not it should continue as an organization. A further meeting agreed to encourage the creation of a new network of communication for individuals to explore the managerial and organizational aspects of the work of the churches and other Christian bodies. This was MODEM.

The word MODEM was originally an acronym for 'managerial and organizational disciplines to enhance ministry'. Subsequently, it became (like British Telecom's 'BT') a term in its own right symbolising a two-way facility whereby insights move freely back and forth between the worlds of management and ministry.

So, who is MODEM? It's a gathering of people who are passionate to see good ministry and good management working together to build up all God's people whether in the church place or in the workplace.

The current Chair of MODEM and its Leadership Committee is the Revd Elizabeth Welch, a former moderator of the West Midlands URC Synod who served as national moderator of the URC from 2001 to 2002.

This book, *101 Great Ideas to Grow Healthy Churches*, is MODEM's fifth to be published by Canterbury Press/SCM and it continues the same format as the previous four, comprising a group of invited contributors under the editorship of myself and my editorial team. The previous four books received much attention, were well reviewed and sold well, especially in the USA, and two of them had to be reprinted.

These four were:

1 *Management and Ministry* (1996) which tackled the issue of churches needing to manage their resources efficiently and effectively.
2 *Leading, Managing, Ministering* (1999) which explored the wider issues of managing in ministry as well as ministering in (secular) management, and of both in leading organizations, secular and sacred.
3 *Creative Church Leadership* (2004) which raised questions crucial for the Christian churches as they face challenges within their own ranks, from other faiths and from a world in need of spiritual wisdom and direction. (John Adair, a leading world authority on leadership, accepted my invitation to become co-editor).
4 *How To Become a Creative Church Leader* (2008). This was the successor to *Creative Church Leadership* and was published in response to many MODEM members' requests for a sequel. The demand for *Creative Church Leadership* had succeeded expectations, selling particularly well in the USA, and its readers were excited by the personal visions of what creative church leadership meant to each of its contributors, and were inspired to want to become one themselves but didn't know how! They pleaded for an authentic and authoritative 'How to Book', a training manual. Hence this fourth book.

May I put on record, as the managing editor of these MODEM publications, my sincere thanks to Christine Smith, Publishing Director of Canterbury Press, for the working partnership we have formed. She has been a continuing source of support, inspiration and ideas to me and the success MODEM books have and continue to have is in no small measure due to her. Thank you, Christine.

As MODEM's national secretary and publications editor, I am contactable by email on – jrn24rcf2003@yahoo.co.uk – or by telephone on 01704 873973 and will be delighted to provide further information about MODEM.

John Nelson